Why Your
History Matters

Strengthen Your Faith by Embracing Your Heritage

Tommy Daugherty

GAZELLE
PRESS

Mobile, Alabama

ISBN 978-1-58169-607-3
For Worldwide Distribution
Printed in the U.S.A.
Gazelle Press
P.O. Box 191540 • Mobile, AL 36619
800-367-8203

Contents

This book is dedicated

to my wife, Suzie,

and our two precious daughters,

Bethany and Stephanie,

who I pray will pass our Christian heritage

on to the next generation.

Introduction

I Didn't Know What I Didn't Know

"How could students raised in the Bible belt know so little of Christian history?" My English Masterpieces professor at the University of Tennessee could not understand why his students were unable to recognize the symbolism and biblical metaphors peppered throughout *Sir Gawain and the Green Knight* during a study of that literary classic. Most of my fellow students laughed along with him and didn't seem to mind their own ignorance, or simply didn't care. His comments struck a nerve with me, though: Why didn't I understand the metaphors present in the poem? Even though I was no student of theology at the time, not even a particularly committed student of the Bible, I kept asking myself, why was I so ignorant? Had I not been paying attention during church? Did it matter?

One thing was certain, my knowledge deficiency was an obstacle I needed to overcome to receive a passing grade in the class. One other thing was certain: The professor had challenged me in a way I'd never expected; he made this six-hundred-year-old poem relevant to my faith.

Written in the fourteenth century, *Sir Gawain and the Green Knight* is a complex poem that depicts corrupt practices in the Church of the day. The Green Knight represents a challenge from the Church of Old, as God intended it, to the Church as it had become. He challenged the values of King Arthur's Court and forced Sir Gawain to come to terms with the shortcomings of the world's greatest court and eventually return to the values of long ago. Some believe it represents the time period between the early Middle Ages and the Reformation.

The professor, who didn't seem to be particularly religious, explained each metaphor to the class; I listened intently. This was amazing; I never realized that English and history could be so interesting! Going into the class, I would have been happy to get a C, but, motivated by the passion of the teacher, I earned an A.

The author of *Sir Gawain* is usually referenced as the Pear Poet and is unknown, but his work is considered a masterpiece of English literature and brilliantly communicates a message to believers, but we must have the ability to understand it. If not for the passion of my teacher, the message of the poem would have been lost on me. Critics of the poem believe the author was a Christian; I agree. Further, this unknown author had a faith that would change the world; his poem would be read and studied by countless students over the years.

In looking back at my college years, so many great things happened. I received an excellent education in my chosen field of study, accounting; I had access to great sports facilities; I met my future wife and the mother of my children; I made several lifelong friends; and I was exposed to some very liberal views of the world. Until recently I would have never included learning to value my Christian heritage among the benefits of attending college. Frequently, college is where a young person's faith goes to die; for me, it was the beginning of a revival of interest in my Christian heritage.

My English Masterpieces professor must also be credited for leading the course with an open mind. He taught the material in the context of the time the poem was written and communicated the core message so that the students would have a better understanding of its significance.

Because of the passion of my professor, I began to understand that "I didn't know what I didn't know" about an important work of literature. I was ignorant of my Christian heritage, but I didn't have a clue this problem existed because I had never been challenged to understand it at a deeper level. Worse, I couldn't have guessed what I was missing. When my mind was finally opened, it was like discovering a new world.

Embracing my heritage caused me to become aware of men and women in history whose faith changed the world; many would die for their cause. My faith was strengthened as I learned of their courage. As believers, we are part of their family. We can be encouraged to know how our Christian ancestors faced dark and difficult times, but we have to first be aware of our ancestors to benefit from their experiences.

Sir Gawain and the Green Knight is an important work, but I never would have known of it, or understood it, had it not been taught to me. *Why Your History Matters* will introduce, or perhaps reintroduce, you to several of our Christian ancestors: Polycarp, Constantine, Joan of Arc, John Wycliffe, William Tyndale, Martin Luther, Charles Dickens, and C. S. Lewis among them. Our Christian heritage is a priceless gift that needs to be shared and passed on to future generations.

As a Christian, we have a heritage that can be traced back to the first believers—and back to Christ. But is Christian heritage in need of a revival? Is it possible that Christians are losing their identity because we have such little knowledge of our past? The definition of *revive* is "to become strong, healthy, or active again, to restore from a depressed, inactive or unused state."

Can there be any doubt in anyone's mind that Christian heritage, or interest in Christian history, is in a depressed state, or is inactive? We must change that condition by locking arms with our ancestors. By embracing our history, we strengthen our faith; we become a link in the chain, a conduit for the heritage to continue to the next generation.

The word *remember* appears in the KJV Bible 148 times, and 166 times in the NIV. There can be no doubt that God thought it important that history be passed from one generation to the next.

In my own life, I had the experience of my mind being opened to a "new world" unexpectedly during an English Masterpieces course over thirty years ago. The "new world" includes ordinary men and women who allowed God to perform extraordinary works in their lives. They are part of our Christian heritage, a link in the chain that is part of where you came from. Their faith changed the world, and so can yours.

Your history is important, and it matters greatly. The information contained in the pages that follow represents only a very small piece of an amazing heritage.

1

We Are Children of Abraham

"Are they Hebrews? So am I. Are they Israelites? So am I. Are they the seed of Abraham? So am I." —Apostle Paul, 2 Corinthians 11:22

As Christians, our family history extends far beyond grandparents or ancestors whom we may have traced through Ancestry.com. Our family history includes an extraordinary lineage of believers, past and present, that can be traced back to the book of Genesis. We have a Jewish heritage, a connection to Abraham. We read in Galatians 3:7: "Know ye therefore that they which are of faith, the same are the children of Abraham" (KJV). According to Paul, believers in Christ are the children of Abraham. To understand the origins of our Christian faith, we must embrace our Jewish heritage.

The mother and earthly father of Christ were Jewish, and Christ is a direct descendant of King David; on that fact we all must agree. The lineage of Christ is traced from His earthly father, Joseph, back to Abraham in the first chapter of the book of Matthew, and from Joseph back to Adam, the son of God, in the third chapter of the book of Luke. Jesus' birth, life, and death are predicted in numerous passages of the Old Testament, hundreds of years before His birth.

It is important that we understand, appreciate, and embrace the books of the Old Testament. We must consider carefully the relevance of scriptures such as Hosea 4:6: "My people are destroyed for lack of knowledge. Because you have rejected knowledge, I also will reject you from being priest for Me; because you have forgotten the law of your God, I also will forget your children." Scriptures such as this get my immediate attention, and they are completely relevant to me today as I have children and a grandchild. God is speaking to us throughout the Old Testament; we must make it a part of our studies and appreciate its place in our heritage.

Until my early twenties, my knowledge of the biblical exodus from Egypt and the Ten Commandments came from watching the movie starring Charlton Heston. Imagine my surprise, years later, when I read the account of Moses contained in the book of Exodus, and didn't find any mention of Moses' relationship with the Pharaoh's niece or even several of the great lines written for Pharaoh and his son. Consider movies released in 2014 that retell the stories of Noah and of the exodus from Egypt; what if these biblically flawed movies comprised the viewer's entire knowledge of those important events in Christian history?

What if, like me, many people received their first impression of biblical events from a source other than the Bible, including cartoons, television, movies, music, and novels? Isn't it important to get exposure to these events, even if not from the Bible? Perhaps, as long as those first impressions do not constitute the *sum total* of our knowledge of Scripture. The concern is that, as much as I enjoyed the movie, there was no depth of knowledge imputed and no understanding given of the context of the event in history.

What do we know about the history of the Old Testament?

During my youth I did not think it was worth my time to read most of the Old Testament, which I thought to be boring and irrelevant to my faith. Ironically, much of the evidence that now affirms my faith in the accuracy of the Old Testament is found among those "boring" portions of Scripture.

In an age when God's Word is questioned and misrepresented, it is important to have confidence in the history of the Old Testament. Not so many years ago, there was a reverence for the ancient books of the Bible. That reverence has now been replaced with apathy and, like history, is at risk of getting lost in translation between generations of believers.

How can we trust the fact that the Bible contains the original words from the authors of the Old Testament? There are hundreds of books on the subject of the inerrant Word of God, but the 1947 discovery of the Dead Sea Scrolls presents some of the strongest evidence for trusting the Old Testament.

The Dead Sea Scrolls

During the spring of 1947, a shepherd threw a stone into some caves in Qumran, which is near the Dead Sea. He heard the sound of breaking pottery, entered the cave for a closer examination, and discovered what may be the greatest archaeological find in the twentieth century. The complete excavation of the caves continued for several years and resulted in the discovery of hundreds of scrolls and fragments.

The Dead Sea Scrolls were believed to have been composed between the third and first centuries BC, then hidden in the caves of Qumran around AD 70, just before the destruction of Jerusalem. The importance of them cannot be overemphasized. Prior to 1947, there were few original documents available to assist scholars in understanding the background of the Bible. When the world realized the manuscripts predated existing evidence by over 1,000 years, there was great anticipation to see if the newly discovered scrolls would rewrite or affirm the Old Testament.

The good news for believers is that the Dead Sea Scrolls consistently affirmed the Old Testament. An excellent summary of the significance of the Dead Sea Scrolls can be found at www.contenderministries.org: "As the importance of the find was realized, the world waited to find out if the scrolls would prove that the Bible had been handed down and translated accurately through the generations. The answer is a resounding yes."

How well do the Dead Sea Scrolls match up with the Old Testament?

Excitement had run high among scholars when it became known in 1948 that a cave near the Dead Sea had produced pre-Masoretic texts of the Bible. Was it possible that we were at last going to see traditions differing seriously from the standard text, which would throw some important light on this hazy period of variant traditions? In some quarters the question was raised with apprehension, especially when news-hungry journalists began to talk about challenging the whole Bible in view of the latest discoveries, but closer examination showed that, on the whole, the differences shown on the first Isaiah scroll were of little account, and could often be explained on the basis of scribal errors, or differing orthography, syntax, or grammatical form. —*John Allegro, not a Christian sympathizer*

The Dead Sea Scrolls represent important evidence in light of the destruction of the Second Temple in AD 70, which resulted in an untold loss of records. Also of note, the discovery of the Dead Sea Scrolls coincided with another significant event in Israel: the establishment of a Jewish State.

On November 29, 1947, the United Nations recommended the adoption of the Partition Plan, and Israel's independence was declared on May 14, 1948.

The Destruction of the Second Temple

On the tenth day of August, AD 70, both the Temple and the city of Jerusalem were destroyed by four legions of Roman soldiers under the command of Titus. There was great looting during the destruction, and a portion of a wall was all that survived. Today that portion is known as the Western Wall, or the Wailing Wall.

Jewish historian Flavius Josephus was present during the destruction and described the event as follows:

> To give a detailed account of their [the Romans] outrageous conduct is impossible, but we may sum it up by saying that no other city has ever endured such horrors, and no generation in history has fathered such wickedness. In the end they brought the whole Hebrew race into contempt in order to make their own impiety seem less outrageous in foreign eyes...

The siege and destruction of Jerusalem, including the Temple, resulted in the deaths of an estimated 1.1 million inhabitants (mostly Jewish), the capture and enslavement of 97,000 people, and the loss of untold numbers of written documents that may have existed in the Temple or elsewhere in the city. It would be approximately 1,900 years before Jews would occupy Jerusalem again, with the establishment of the Jewish State in 1947.

The Canonization of the Old Testament

The Canon (from the Greek word *kanon*, meaning "rule") of Scripture refers to those writings believed to be authoritative and divinely inspired. For consideration for inclusion in the Scriptures, the primary criterion was the author's relationship with God and the consistency of the book with earlier revelations from God. No one questioned that Moses spoke God's words, so the five books of the Pentateuch were accepted long before other books.

The Pentateuch, or Torah, which is the first five books of the Bible as compiled by Moses, refers to Genesis, Exodus, Leviticus, Numbers, and

Deuteronomy—also referred to as "The Law." The five books originally formed a single scroll, but they were divided into five individual books perhaps during the process of preparing the Septuagint by the Greek translators.

Over the course of time, other books, along with the Pentateuch, were placed in the Tabernacle or Temple; these were known as the Sacred Writings. During the Babylonian captivity (around 600 BC), the Sacred Writings were scattered and many copies were destroyed. After the return from seventy years of captivity, Ezra reassembled scattered copies and restored them as a complete group to their place in the Temple.

The process of copying the scrolls was painstaking and executed with great diligence by the Jewish scribes. If even the slightest mistake was made in copying, such as allowing two letters to touch each other, they destroyed the complete panel and also the panel it had touched in the scroll.

The Septuagint

Considered by some to be the most important and influential translation ever completed, the Septuagint is the oldest translation of the Old Testament. King Ptolemy of Egypt endeavored to preserve all wisdom of the world in the Library of Alexandria and ordered that work on the translation begin during the third century BC. To preserve the Jewish Scriptures he entreated King Herod to send him the scrolls of the Old Testament, but he found them written in the Hebrew language. In order to translate them into the common Greek language for placement in the library, the king commissioned seventy-two scholars from Jerusalem, six from each of the twelve tribes of Israel. King Ptolemy also released 100,000 Jewish slaves to entice King Herod to agree to the translation.

The Egyptian king placed the translation team in guarded, separate areas to work independently. Remarkably (miraculously?) the first five books (the Pentateuch) were completed in seventy-two days. The books produced independently by the translators employed the same use of words and gave the same meaning to the text. The men appointed as guards were interviewed and each testified to the same accuracy, and first-century historians Philo and Josephus confirmed the events.

The Septuagint contains the standard thirty-nine books of the Old Testament canon, as well as certain Apocryphal books. The Apocryphal books were included in the Septuagint for historical and religious purposes, but they are not recognized by Protestant Christians or Orthodox Jews as canonical (inspired by God), although the Roman Catholic Church and the Orthodox Church include most of the Apocryphal books.

The Septuagint is important because it was a source of the Old Testament for Christians during the early centuries AD, as many early Christians spoke and read Greek. The New Testament writers relied heavily on the Septuagint translation, as a majority of Old Testament quotes cited in the New Testament are taken directly from the Septuagint. Before the discovery of the Dead Sea Scrolls, the earliest known manuscripts of the Old Testament were not Hebrew, but copies of the Septuagint. The Septuagint and the Dead Sea Scrolls establish a very dramatic piece of evidence for Christianity—that the Old Testament prophecies of the coming Messiah unquestionably predated the time that Jesus Christ walked the earth.

The Catholic and Orthodox Christian Bibles continue to make use of the Septuagint; the Protestant Bible makes use of the Masoretic Text.

The Masoretic Text

Produced by the Masoretes between the sixth and tenth centuries AD, the Masoretic Text is the authoritative Hebrew text of the Jewish Bible. The Masoretes were Rabbinic scribe-scholars who worked to preserve the original Hebrew texts and their society. The Masoretic Text is considered to be a more accurate translation of the original books of the Old Testament and was used in the King James Version.

What Bible Did Jesus Use?

There is some debate as to whether Jesus might have used the Septuagint as His source of scripture, which was available at the time and used by Greek-speaking Israelites as well as a million people living in Alexandria, Egypt. There is evidence that Jesus referred to several texts, including the Masoretic, Septuagint, and Aramaic. Although there is no unanimous answer to this question, we know that Jesus referred to the Old Testament Scriptures in three parts: the Law, the Prophets, and the Psalms (Luke 24:44).

In *The Canon Debate*, Lee McDonald and James Sanders present a thorough study of quotations of Jesus, tracing them to various texts available during the period. The authors conclude that Jesus did not recognize a specific text form of scripture.

Some supporters of the Septuagint believe that the Masoretic Text is the product of a deliberate effort by the Jews to discredit Christianity by replacing the original Hebrew texts with newer Hebrew translations. The conspiracy theory sets forth that the newer translations altered verses that supported the Christian view of Christ as the Messiah. More information on the Masoretic Text can be found at the website entitled: www.biblebelievers.org.au/masoret.htm.

Morsels of the Old Testament

The Old Testament is the very foundation of the New Testament; remember Jesus' words:

Do not think that I came to destroy the Law or the Prophets. I did not come to destroy but to fulfill. —Matthew 5:17

In his book *30 Days to Understanding the Bible*, Max Anders divides the Old Testament into nine main eras; Creation, Patriarch, Exodus, Conquest, Judges, Kingdom, Exile, Return, and Silence.

A basic understanding of Genesis is so very important in order to appreciate the Bible; perhaps this explains why various portions have been under attack since the early centuries. The attacks continue to this day (see Dr. Henry Morris's book *The Long War Against God*).

The book of Genesis includes the biblical account of creation, including the origin of the first man, woman, and the account of their children. Genesis also includes God's plan for marriage, Noah's flood, and the Tower of Babel (which explains the various languages and people groups in the world today). In Genesis we read about the accounts of Abraham, Ishmael, Isaac, Jacob (later named Israel), and Joseph.

Before we consider a view of history other than biblical, we need to consider the slippery slope upon which we are embarking. Entire ministries have been established dedicated to providing evidence confirming the biblical accounts depicted in Genesis as well as advising of the dangers to a person's faith when accepting non-biblical explanations. Visit the Answers in Genesis website at www.answersingenesis.org for more information.

Among the challenges to the content of Genesis is the question, "Was there an actual Adam?" A short answer to that is taken from a few scriptures in the New Testament, found in Luke, chapter 3, and beginning with verse 23, and continuing thru verse 38. One of two lineages of Christ is detailed in this chapter. Working backward in the line of Christ includes Joseph (his earthly father), David (the son of Jesse), Judah (the son of Joseph), Noah (the son of Lamech), Seth (the son of Adam), and Adam (the son of God).

Paul writes about Adam in 1 Corinthians 15:45: "And so it is written, 'The first man Adam became a living being.' The last Adam became a life-giving spirit."

The Old Testament continues with the history of God's chosen people in the book of Exodus, including the deliverance of the Hebrews from the Egyptians and the beginning of Passover, the crossing of the Red Sea, and the Ten Commandments. Also included is the wandering in the desert, the conquest of the Promised Land, the period of the Judges, the Kings of Israel, the exile period (for seventy years the nation Israel is in captivity), the return, and finally four hundred years of silence between the last book of the Old Testament and the birth of Christ.

The biblical accounts of God's dealing with the rebellious nation of Israel hold a lot of lessons for us today. In the same way we study the rise and fall of Rome, leaders of nations can study the history of Israel for answers to problems faced in the present age, as most can be traced to a common source: disobedience to and a disregard of a sovereign God.

The most common verse I hear today regarding the state of things in the world comes from the book of Judges. The context is the period after the Exodus from Egypt, after crossing into the Promised Land. Moses and Joshua are now dead. God provided several judges, including Deborah and Samson, but they are now dead. This is in the time before King David. During those days people were no longer turning to God for answers; they had forgotten their own history.

> *In those days there was no king in Israel; everyone did what was right in his own eyes.* —Judges 21:25

The Ten Commandments

Is the Old Testament still relevant? There should be no doubt that the Old Testament is as relevant today as it has ever been to any people group.

Consider carefully the Ten Commandments given to Moses by God on Mount Sinai. They represent God's plan for the newly born nation of Israel:

> *I am the LORD your God, who brought you out of the land of Egypt, out of the house of bondage. You shall have no other gods before Me. You shall not make for yourself a carved image... You shall not take the name of the LORD your God in vain... Remember the Sabbath day, to keep it holy... Honor your father and your mother... You shall not murder. You shall not commit adultery. You shall not steal. You shall not bear false witness against your neighbor. You shall not covet your neighbor's house, you shall not covet your neighbor's wife....* —Exodus 20:2–17

Much attention is paid to the evidence that refutes the biblical accounts of history as well as bestselling books of fiction (presented as fact), but little attention is given to the evidence that supports the biblical accounts of history. In a day and age when people may be getting their history lessons from movies or books of fiction, there is little interest in devoting time to reading the Old Testament. The Old Testament should be considered the cornerstone in building our knowledge of Christian history and can enrich your prayer life.

The following list contains a few examples of Old Testament prophecy that were fulfilled during the time period of the Old Testament that may provide some motivation to dig a little deeper and learn a little more.

Old Testament Prophecies Fulfilled during Old Testament Times

The destruction of Tyre was accurately foretold approximately four hundred years before it occurred, when the prophet Amos made the following prediction:

> *Thus says the LORD: For three transgressions of Tyre, and for four, I will not turn away its punishment, because they delivered up the whole captivity to Edom, and did not remember the covenant of brotherhood. But I will send a fire upon the wall of Tyre, which shall devour its palaces.*
> —Amos 1:9–10

9

The prophecy of Amos was fulfilled in BC 586–573, when Babylonian King Nebuchadnezzar attacked the mainland of Tyre, and in BC 333–332, when Alexander the Great conquered the island of Tyre.

Additional prophecies about the destruction of Tyre can be found in the book of Ezekiel, written between BC 587 and 586. The prophet Ezekiel predicted that Tyre's stones, timber, and soil would be cast into the sea, that Tyre would lose its power over the sea, and that Tyre would never be rebuilt. All of these prophecies were fulfilled when Alexander the Great conquered the city by building a land bridge to reach the inhabitants at a location off-shore after they had moved there. Alexander's fulfillment of Ezekiel's prophecy should make even the most skeptical person sit up and take notice.

The historically accurate story of Tyre is amazing, yet it is doubtful many people today even know of it. And there is another prophecy about the fall of a great city; that city was Nineveh.

The prophet Jonah was directed by God to go to the city of Nineveh and preach, as its wickedness had come up before Him. Jonah rebelled against God and sailed for Tarshish instead. A great storm came and the crew was afraid of perishing, but Jonah advised them to throw him overboard and the sea would grow calm again. A great fish came and swallowed Jonah and carried him to Nineveh, where he preached God's Word. Amazingly the king and people of Nineveh repented and God spared them. Jonah was not pleased with this outcome, but God reminded him that there should be concern for the city of Nineveh, where there were more than 120,000 people who could not tell their right hand from their left hand. So the great city of Nineveh was spared from the wrath of God as a result of their repentance around BC 781.

In BC 614, Nineveh served as the capital of the Assyrian Empire and may have been the most powerful city of the ancient world. The prophet Nahum prophesied about the destruction of Nineveh, including the method of its destruction, fire (Nahum 3:15). In BC 612, the city of Nineveh was destroyed, marking the end of the Assyrian Empire. The ruins of Nineveh were unearthed during the 1800s, and the archaeologists found a layer of ash covering the ruins.

One of the most sobering prophecies in the Old Testament can be found in the book of Daniel. Entire books are devoted to the study of the prophecies of Daniel; this chapter will only cover the "writing on the wall." The fifth chapter of the book of Daniel tells of a great party in which the king was praising the gods of gold and silver, bronze and iron, wood and stone. Then suddenly the fingers of a man's hand appeared and wrote on the plaster of the wall, "MENE, MENE, TEKEL, UPHARSIN" (verse 25).

None of the king's advisors could interpret the writing, and soon Daniel was summoned. Beginning with verse 22 of chapter 5 in the book of Daniel, we learn that the king had praised the gods of gold and silver, and yet not glorified the God who held his very breath in His hand.

Here are the meanings of the words inscribed on the palace wall: "MENE: God has numbered your kingdom, and finished it, TEKEL: You have been weighed in the balances, and been found wanting, UPHARSIN: Your kingdom has been divided, and given to the Medes and Persians. That very night Belshazzar, king of the Chaldeans, was slain." This meaning is found in Daniel 5:26–30.

The Ark of the Covenant

During my junior year in college (1981), the biggest movie was *Raiders of the Lost Ark*. I don't remember being clear on what the Ark of the Covenant was during that period of my life, but the movie was exciting and had strong religious overtones related to the significance of it. The basic story was that Hitler desired to find the Ark, which was believed to contain the actual tablets associated with Moses and the Ten Commandments. Hitler believed an army carrying the Ark could defeat any foe.

Professor Henry (Indiana) Jones is recruited by two government agents who don't understand what Hitler is looking for. They are not familiar with the Ark, or that the Hebrews carried it ahead of them when defeating Jericho and other cities while taking their "Promised Land." During their meeting Indiana Jones even asked them if they had ever gone to Sunday school. Indiana Jones is not a believer, but he knows the history of the Ark. This reminded me of my English Masterpieces professor who was not a believer and was surprised by the ignorance of his class in the "Bible Belt." Indiana Jones is hired by the United States government to find the Ark of the Covenant before the Nazis can find it, on the outside chance that the item does have supernatural powers.

Indiana Jones is the first to find the Ark, but he loses it to his arch-enemy, fellow archaeologist Rene Belloq, who has been hired by the Nazis. Jones catches up to him toward the end of the movie and threatens to blow it up if they don't release his girlfriend, Marion Ravenwood. Belloq called his bluff and told him to blow the Ark back to God and that they were only passing through history, while the Ark was part of real history. In the end, Indiana Jones prevails and the Nazis who participated in a ceremony opening the Ark are all destroyed by the powers released when it is opened. The Ark is then stored in an undisclosed location, where it resides to this day (per the movie).

What is the real story behind the Ark of the Covenant? Did it really exist? Did it have supernatural powers? Do we know where it is today? The answers begin in the book of Exodus, chapter 25, where God instructs the Hebrews to build the Ark. God gives the Hebrews specific instructions: It is to be made with acacia wood and overlaid with gold. The Ark contained the stone tablets bearing the inscription of the Ten Commandments, as well as the staff of Aaron (Moses' brother) and a golden jar of manna. God fed the Hebrews with manna during their forty years of wandering in the desert.

When the Israelites were traveling, they carried the Ark ahead of them and it was the center of their worship when not traveling. After their time of wandering in the desert (due to their disobedience to God), the Israelites were directed to take Jericho, a large fortified city. Joshua was leading the Israelites after Moses was not allowed to enter the Promised Land, and God directed him to march around the city once each day for six days, and on the seventh day to march around the city seven times with the priests blowing their trumpets. After the priests sounded a long blast, the people were to shout, and the walls would collapse, which is exactly what happened.

At one point in its history, the Ark was captured by the Philistines during a defeat of the Israelites. It was taken to their capital city of Ashdod, where it was placed in the temple of their god, Dagon. The next day they found their idol fallen on its face, so they replaced it. The next day they found the new statue of Dagon decapitated, and soon after the entire city was struck by the plague. The Philistines then moved the Ark to the city of Gath, then to Ekron, but wherever the Ark was placed, that city was struck by the plague.

After seven months, the Philistines returned the Ark to Israel along with a guilt offering in hopes that God would lift His hand from them. They were aware of the plagues of Egypt. The historical account of the capture and return of the Ark of the Covenant is found in the fifth and sixth chapters of 1 Samuel in the Bible. The Ark remained with Israel until the destruction of the Temple by the Babylonian Empire, led by Nebuchadnezzar.

From the time the Ark was constructed until the destruction of the Temple approximately 850 years passed (about BC 1440–586). Where is it today? No one knows. Two fascinating possibilities are the Church of St. Mary of Zion in Axum, Ethiopia, where it could be guarded by a monk, or it may be buried in the Temple Mount. Archaeologist Leen Ritmeyer, who has conducted research on the Temple Mount and inside the Dome of the Rock, postulates that the Ark may be buried deep inside the Temple Mount. However, it is unlikely that any excavation will ever be allowed by Muslim or Israeli authorities.

To the Jews, the Ark of the Covenant was the most important symbol of their faith. Regarding the possible whereabouts of the Ark, we must be aware of the words of the prophet Jeremiah (who prophesied about the destruction of Judah from BC 626 to about BC 586):

> *Then it shall come to pass, when you are multiplied and increased in the land in those days," says the LORD, "that they will say no more, 'The ark of the covenant of the LORD.' It shall not come to mind, nor shall they remember it, nor shall they visit it, nor shall it be made anymore.*
>
> —Jeremiah 3:16

The book of Job is considered by many scholars to be the oldest book in the Bible. It provides a lesson to humanity that things aren't always as they seem, that God is God and we shouldn't presume to understand His plans. Job encounters significant tragedy in his life due to no fault of his own. His counselors believe that he is experiencing evil, that he must have done something to warrant God's punishment. God confronts Job and his counselors at the end of the book and sets them straight, however. In chapter 38, verse 4, God asks of Job, "Where were you when I laid the foundations of the earth? Tell Me, if you have understanding."

As children of Abraham, we share a history that matters. If Christians forsake the Old Testament, we risk losing any real understanding of the

New Testament. If we forsake our Jewish heritage, we risk losing our connection to Christ. It is through Christ that we are adopted into the family of Abraham to share God's promise. Abraham, Isaac, Jacob, and Joseph are patriarchs of our Christian family. Gaining an understanding of them will only strengthen our faith, but failing to do so could greatly weaken our faith.

2

Preparing the Way for the Word

The four-hundred-year period of time between the last book of the Old Testament, Malachi, and the birth of Christ, is considered by some as a "period of silence" from God. While there is no biblical record of God speaking through His prophets during this period, research reveals that at least two significant events occurred that would greatly improve the ability of believers to later spread the message of Christ. God was preparing a way for His Word to be spread. To use a modern-era analogy, God used these events to develop the equivalent of an Internet, a foundation that would allow mass communication.

First, Alexander the Great's conquest of the world resulted in the development of a common language, Greek. Second, Rome's conquest of the world resulted in the development of a system of roads throughout their empire. The combination of a common language and a system of roads is no less significant for that time period than the development of the Internet is today. One could certainly argue that God was preparing the world for the message of His Son by creating His own "Internet" for that day and age. Until recently I never seriously considered events during the four hundred years prior to the birth of Christ. Again, I didn't know what I didn't know, and I wasn't looking to see God's hand at work in history.

Increasing our knowledge of history is like adding reinforcing rods and concrete to the foundation of a building; the more we learn of the history of our faith, our Church, and our family, the better we understand ourselves. Knowledge of history equips us to deal with the bumps and twists we encounter in our own journey through life.

In Knoxville, Tennessee, there is a popular show, *The Heartland Series*, which depicts scenes and memories from the past. The style of the host is very respectful, patient, and attentive when interviewing guests, who are frequently senior citizens. In my mind, the popularity of the series is related to people's interest in their past, being reminded of traditions and memories that would otherwise be forgotten.

So of what importance are the events that occurred during the four hundred years of silence? To answer this question I rely heavily upon information obtained from www.templemount.org.

We must understand the situation in Jerusalem during the writing of the book of Malachi. Solomon's Temple, first destroyed in BC 586, had been rebuilt, although the new temple was much smaller. The priests were descendants of Aaron. There was no one left from the line of David on the throne of Judah, nor was there a king of Israel, as the nation of Israel was under the rule of Persia. To quote www.templemount.com: "God allowed a period of time for the teachings of the Old Testament to penetrate throughout the world." Babylon was the world power when the prophet Malachi was writing, which was succeeded by the Medio-Persian empire, as was prophesied by the prophet Daniel (Daniel 7:5).

During the time when the Persian Empire was at its height, a man named Philip of Macedon became a leader and united his country of Macedonia. The son of Philip of Macedon became one of the great leaders in world history: Alexander the Great. In BC 330, Alexander the Great led the armies of Greece to victory over the Persians, removing Persia from power and shifting the center of world power to Greece. Within a year Alexander would lead his armies into Egypt with a siege of Jerusalem planned along the way.

Alexander the Great and Jerusalem

As the armies of Greece approached Jerusalem, the high priest at the time was Jaddua (mentioned in Nehemiah 12:11, 22) who, along with a host of other priests, met Alexander before he reached Jerusalem and showed him the writings of Daniel. According to the Jewish historian Josephus, Alexander left his armies and met the priests; he told them he had experienced a vision the night before in which God had shown him an old man, robed in white, who would show him something of great significance. Josephus writes that Jaddua then opened the prophecies of Daniel to Alexander, who was overwhelmed by the accuracy of the predictions made by the prophet. He then promised he would save Jerusalem from siege.

The prophet Daniel predicted the conquests of Alexander the Great around BC 600, which was several hundred years before Alexander's birth.

Daniel prophesied that someone would come from the West and smash the power of Medio-Persia and go on to conquer the world. Alexander would accomplish that by the age of thirty-three. He also conquered Egypt, and in BC 331, he created the city of Alexandria, which was designed to be the hub of Greek culture.

Alexandria was the capital of Hellenistic, Roman, and Byzantine Egypt for nearly one thousand years, until the Muslim conquest of Egypt in AD 641. Hellenistic Alexandria was known for the Lighthouse of Alexandria, one of the seven wonders of the ancient world, and for its Great Library (the largest in the ancient world).

From the expansion of Greek culture, we have an understanding as to why the people of Jesus' day spoke and wrote in Greek. We also need to be aware of the importance of the Greek language, which has been described as a "beautiful, rich, and harmonious" instrument of communication. The conquests of Alexander the Great resulted in the spread of the Greek language.

Was God preparing the world for the spread of His Gospel and using the Greek language as a tool? Some scholars consider it significant that Paul wrote his letter to the Christians in Rome in Greek, rather than Latin, as the Roman Empire was culturally a Greek world at the time.

Alexander died in BC 323 at the age of thirty-three, and he left no heirs to take over his throne. Eventually the four generals who had led Alexander's armies divided the kingdom between themselves; Ptolemy took over Egypt and other northern African countries. Palestine was annexed by Egypt and under Ptolemy's rule. A general named Seleucus took over Syria, which was to the north of Palestine. During the coming years there was frequent conflict between Egypt and Syria with Palestine caught in the middle. The eleventh chapter of Daniel gives an account of the years of conflict between the king of the north (Syria) and the king of the south (Egypt). H. A. Ironside's book, *The 400 Silent Years,* details these events.

Pharisees and Sadducees

During this time Grecian influence was becoming strong in Palestine, and many people were eager to bring the Grecian culture into Jerusalem. Those seeking to bring in the Grecian culture were called Hellenists; they sought to liberalize Jewish laws. Others resisted the foreign influence and sought to preserve traditions of the past; this group became known as the

Pharisees, which means "to separate." The Pharisees separated from the others in order to preserve the Jewish traditions; in their attempt to accomplish this, they established rules and rigid requirements. Jesus had harsh words for the Pharisees, whom He called hypocrites, for keeping the outward form of the law while violating the spirit of the law.

The Hellenists became more influential in the political process, and they formed the party that became known as the Sadducees, which was much more liberal than the Pharisees. It should be noted that the Sadducees did not believe in supernatural intervention, and time and again they questioned Jesus on this subject. For example, in Matthew 22:23–33, Jesus was questioned by the Sadducees regarding marriage and the resurrection as it relates to a woman who had been widowed several times.

It was during the time of Egyptian rule that the Septuagint translation was prepared. This first ever Greek translation of the Hebrew Scriptures is still in existence today and used in parts of the world. Unfortunately, the Egyptians lost possession of Palestine around BC 203 to Syria, which was under the rule of Antiochus the Great. His son, Antiochus Epiphanes, would eventually succeed his father and brother and would become one of the most violent and vicious persecutors of Jews of all time.

The Antichrist of the Old Testament

Antiochus Epiphanes would fulfill some of the prophecies of Daniel with respect to the coming of one who would be a "contemptible person" and a "vile king." Among the detestable acts he committed upon the people of Jerusalem was to depose the high priest and then sell the priesthood. This ended the long line of succession that could be traced back to Aaron and the Exodus. Later he invaded Egypt, again throwing Palestine into the middle of conflict. While he was in Egypt it was reported back to Jerusalem that Antiochus had been killed. Upon hearing of his death, the people of Jerusalem were overjoyed and overthrew the priest who had been appointed by Antiochus.

Sadly for the inhabitants of Jerusalem, Antiochus had not been killed in Egypt as they had heard. Upon hearing of the actions taken by the Jews when they thought he had perished, he assembled his armies and went to Jerusalem to vent his wrath. In three days of fighting, forty thousand people perished. Even worse, Antiochus entered the Holy of Holies and desecrated the temple. He sacrificed a sow (a female pig) upon the altar, made a broth from the unclean animal, and sprinkled it around the temple, thus completely violating it.

It might not be possible for us to comprehend how detestable the act was that Antiochus committed upon the temple in the eyes of the Jews. The act of desecration was referred to by Jesus as the "desolating sacrilege," predicted by Daniel (Matthew 24:15), and is a sign of things that have not yet come when the Antichrist enters the temple. The prophet Daniel predicted that the sanctuary would be polluted for 2,300 days (Daniel 8:14). This prophecy was fulfilled by Antiochus, as it took 2,300 days for the temple to be cleansed after he defiled it.

Is your heart breaking for the people of Jerusalem? Jerusalem is the most captured city in all of history, and it has been ravished, burned, and destroyed twenty-seven times. Palestine is the most-fought-over country in the world. The four hundred years preceding the birth of Christ represents an important part of Christian history and is worth knowing.

The temple was cleansed under the leadership of a person famous in Jewish history, but who should also be known to Christians, Judas Maccabaeus. Judas was of the priestly line and, along with his father and four brothers, defied the Syrian king and rallied the Israelites. In a series of battles, in which the Israelites were outnumbered, they defeated the forces of the Syrian king and recaptured Jerusalem. Cleansing of the temple was completed on the twenty-fifth of December BC 164, known as the Day of Dedication. The Day of Dedication is celebrated to this very day.

The years following the deposition of the Syrian king would be known as the Days of the Maccabees, during which there was no foreign domination of Jerusalem. Also during this time a new power rose in the west— Rome. This book will not cover the battles leading up to how Jerusalem came under the control of the Roman Empire in BC 63. However, the Roman Senate appointed the procurator of Judea, who in turn made his two sons the kings of Galilee and Judea. The king of Judea was Herod. This is the same Herod referenced in Matthew 2:1–2, who asks, "Where is He who has been born King of the Jews?" Herod is also a descendant of Esau; this should be worth noting, as we know the descendants of Esau had no love for the descendants of Jacob.

There are at least two reasons the four hundred years of God's silence was vastly important to the spread of Christianity: 1) a common language

(Greek) was spread throughout the world, making it easier for the people to read the New Testament, and 2) the Romans constructed roads, making it easier for the Gospel to spread. A common language and roads connecting cities: God was preparing the way for His Word to be spread.

How important is the interstate road system in the United States? Did the Internet help to facilitate global communication? We must think on this scale to appreciate the importance of the Greeks and Romans in facilitating communication, part of our heritage.

3

"The Word Became Flesh"

Perhaps the most exciting and hope-filled words ever written can be found in John 1:14: "The Word became flesh and dwelt among us." The birth of the Savior of the world was accurately predicted 1,200 years before His birth.

Prophecies related to the life of Christ were relatively unknown to me when I was in college. Aside from singing about them at Christmas, it didn't really sink in that events about Jesus' life had been foretold several hundred years before His birth. However, I was fortunate to have an excellent Sunday school teacher during my "young married couples" years, who did his homework on the subject of fulfillment of prophecy that occurred with the birth of Jesus.

An underlying theme of this book is that I have been blessed with great teachers, who had a visible passion in the subjects they were teaching. It is said that passion persuades; no doubt apathy has the opposite effect. Thinking back, my ignorance of Old Testament prophecies about Christ weakened my faith, while gaining an understanding of them strengthened my faith. I was astounded to learn that prophets were able to predict details of the birth, life, ministry, and death of Christ hundreds of years before they occurred.

The following is a listing of selected verses from the Bible that reflect the fulfillment of prophecies.

Prophecies More Than 1,200 Years Before Christ

The book of Genesis tells us that the coming Messiah would be born of a woman (Genesis 3:15), from the line of Abraham (Genesis 12:3 and 22:18), and a descendant of Isaac (Genesis 17:19 and 21:12). Other prophecies include the Messiah being a descendant of Jacob (Numbers 24:17), from the tribe of Judah (Genesis 49:10), a firstborn son, and sanctified (Exodus 13:2, Numbers 3:13 and 8:17). Referring to the death of Christ, the prophecies declare that He would be hung upon a tree as a curse for us (Deuteronomy 21:23) and that no bone of His body would be broken (Exodus 12:46).

Prophecies More Than 800 Years before Christ

More than 800 years before His birth, Samuel prophesied that Jesus would be from the line of David (2 Samuel 7:12–13). Concerning His death, we read in Psalms that Jesus would be betrayed by a close friend (Psalm 41:9), would thirst, would be given gall and vinegar (Psalm 22:15 and 69:20–22), would be pierced in His hands and feet (Psalm 22:16), and would have His garments gambled for (Psalm 22:18).

Prophecies More Than 500 Years before Christ

Detailed in the verses that follow, written more than 500 years before His birth, prophets predicted where He would be born, that children would be massacred because of His birth, that He would live in Egypt for a time, that He would enter Jerusalem on a donkey, and that He would be despised and rejected, just to name a few. It is vital that we understand that meticulous details of the life of Christ were documented in the canonized Old Testament hundreds of years before His birth. Below is evidence that the birth of Christ was chronicled about 700 years before the event.

> *But you, Bethlehem Ephrathah, though you are little among the thousands of Judah, yet out of you shall come forth to Me the One to be Ruler in Israel, whose goings forth are from of old, from everlasting.* —Micah 5:2

In Matthew 2:16–18 we read that King Herod was so upset when he realized that the Magi had outwitted him and not identified the newborn King, that he ordered all boys in Bethlehem and its vicinity who were two years old and under be killed. The massacre of the children was predicted over 600 years earlier by the prophet Jeremiah:

> *Thus says the LORD: "A voice was heard in Ramah, Lamentation and bitter weeping, Rachel weeping for her children, refusing to be comforted for her children, because they are no more."* —Jeremiah 31:15

Jesus is called the "Lamb of God," and He represents the sacrifice for our sins so that we can spend eternity with God. In an attempt to kill Christ before He could grow and fulfill His purpose, Herod was willing to murder innocent children. This event is similar to the account of Moses, who was spared during a time in Egypt when Pharaoh ordered that every Israelite boy who was born must be thrown into the river.

We know that Mary and Joseph were warned to flee to Egypt to escape the murder of the children born in Bethlehem, where they stayed until the death of Herod. The prophet Hosea foretold their return from Egypt more than 700 years before it happened. Jesus, the Son of God, was called out of Egypt, just as the nation of Israel was called out of Egypt approximately 1,500 years earlier.

We would be remiss if we failed to mention the prophecy of the one who was to come before Christ to "prepare the way before Him." Approximately BC 465, the prophet Malachi wrote of a messenger who would prepare the way, that prophecy being fulfilled by John the Baptist. The prophet Isaiah also predicted John the Baptist's role around BC 700:

The voice of one crying in the wilderness: "Prepare the way of the LORD; make straight in the desert a highway for our God." —Isaiah 40:3

John the Baptist was a cousin of Jesus, as John's mother, Elizabeth, was a cousin of Mary, the mother of Jesus. John preached repentance in the area of Judea (Matthew 3:1), and he baptized Jesus, who said of John the Baptist, "Assuredly, I say to you, among those born of women there has not risen one greater than John the Baptist; but he who is least in the kingdom of heaven is greater than he" (Matthew 11:11).

The phrase "bringing someone's head on a platter" can actually be traced to the beheading of John the Baptist by King Herod. The account of the arrest and subsequent beheading of John the Baptist can be found in Matthew 14:1–12.

The three- to four-year ministry of Jesus is recorded in the four gospels of the New Testament. Countless books have been authored about Christ and the effects of His world-changing ministry. This book is not intended to cover His ministry and teachings, but simply to provide enough information to spark an interest to learn more. The best way to learn about Christ is to read the four gospels of the New Testament: Matthew, Mark,

Luke, and John. Then read the rest of the New Testament, and then the Old Testament.

Regarding prayer, in the sixth chapter of the book of Matthew, Jesus instructed us to pray privately, and not to ramble in long, babbling words.

In this manner, therefore, pray: Our Father in heaven, hallowed be Your name. Your kingdom come. Your will be done On earth as it is in heaven. Give us this day our daily bread. And forgive us our debts, As we forgive our debtors. And do not lead us into temptation, But deliver us from the evil one. For Yours is the kingdom and the power and the glory forever. Amen.
—Matthew 6:9–13

Has better counsel ever been given by any living person than from Jesus? The fifth, sixth, and seventh chapters of Matthew provide counsel on the subjects of the Jewish law, murder, divorce, caring for the needy, worrying, judging others, and seeking God.

We now come to that great event in history that marked the fulfillment of the ancient prophecies, and provided the great sacrifice by both the Creator and His only begotten Son. Because of this event, you and I know that we are loved beyond comprehension, that there is purpose to life, and that we have a great hope. Prior to His entry into Jerusalem, Jesus advised the twelve disciples:

Behold, we are going up to Jerusalem, and the Son of Man will be betrayed to the chief priests and to the scribes; and they will condemn Him to death, and deliver Him to the Gentiles to mock and to scourge and to crucify. And the third day He will rise again.
—Matthew 20:18–19

The Night before the Crucifixion

In writing about the life of Christ, I think of the scribes who recorded the Old Testament with such meticulous care and in reverent prayer; they sincerely believed in the importance of their work. Great books and movies have attempted to capture the last hours of Jesus' life leading up to His crucifixion, all with one overarching theme: Christ loved us to the point of death. The apostle John records the events of that evening in the gospel bearing his name, beginning with Chapter 13.

Jesus knew that the time had come for Him to leave this world and go to the Father.

Now before the Feast of the Passover, when Jesus knew that His hour had come that He should depart from this world to the Father, having loved His own who were in the world, He loved them to the end.   —John 13:1

Jesus washed the feet of His disciples, including Judas, in an act of absolute humility. The custom in Jesus' day was that the lowliest servant would perform the foot washing. But Jesus instructed them to wash each other's feet. Jesus again predicted His betrayal, quoting Psalm 41:9, referring to Judas, who would break bread with Him during the Feast of the Passover they were about to observe.

During the Feast of the Passover the disciples were confused as to whom Jesus was referring to as the one who would betray Him. In my own life, I ponder how many times I have betrayed the Lord, even when He has warned me in advance, as He did for Judas, telling him: "What you do, do quickly." The other disciples did not understand why Jesus said this to Judas or why Judas left.

Jesus informed Peter that Satan had desired to "sift him as wheat," but Jesus had prayed for him that his faith would not fail. Peter responded to Jesus by saying that he was ready to go with Jesus both to prison and to death.

Imagine Christ Himself praying that Satan would not have you; this is the very message we need to bring the world. How would you respond if you were put in Peter's position? Does God care whether you come to repentance? Consider the following:

The Lord is not slack concerning His promise, as some count slackness, but is longsuffering toward us, not willing that any should perish but that all should come to repentance.   —2 Peter 3:9

Jesus informed Peter that before the rooster crowed that day, he would deny three times that he knew His Savior. I imagine that to Peter it would have seemed impossible to deny Jesus once, much less three times before daybreak. What could possibly happen to cause him to deny his Lord? But later you will read that Jesus' prediction about Peter came true.

In the record of the final hours of Christ, it is clear that His main concern was for those being left behind, not for His own life or to be spared the torture to come. In the gospel of John we read of the love Christ had for the disciples during the final hours before the cross as He shared words of comfort with them:

> *"Let not your heart be troubled; you believe in God, believe also in Me. In My Father's house are many mansions: if it were not so, I would have told you. I go to prepare a place for you. And if I go and prepare a place for you, I will come again and receive you to Myself; that where I am, there you may be also."* —John 14:1–3

What great encouragement and hope for the future we are given by the words of Christ as He prepared to fulfill God's plan for the world. When questioned by Thomas about His destination and the way to get there, Jesus delivered a warning that would forever divide mankind. Even in typing the words, I realize the power and consequences of their meaning and the effect they had on the next two thousand years of history:

> *Jesus said to him, "I am the way, the truth, and the life. No one comes to the Father except through Me."* —John 14:6

> *"Greater love has no one than this, than to lay down one's life for his friends."* —John 15:13

Incredibly, Jesus told the disciples over and over again of events that would occur in just a few hours, realizing the extreme fear they would experience after the crucifixion. After the Feast of the Passover, they went out to the Mount of Olives, just outside of Jerusalem, where Jesus went to pray alone in the Garden of Gethsemane. The words of Jesus' prayer reveal the meaning of eternal life, His great concern for the disciples, and His prayer for those who would believe as a result of His message.

> *"And this is eternal life, that they may know You, the only true God, and Jesus Christ whom You have sent. I have glorified You on the earth. I have finished the work which You have given Me to do. And now, O Father, glorify Me together with Yourself, with the glory which I had with You before the world was."* —John 17:3–5

Speaking of His disciples:

"I have given them Your word; and the world has hated them because they are not of the world, just as I am not of the world. I do not pray that You should take them out of the world, but that You should keep them from the evil one." —John 17:14–15

Speaking of those who would believe later:

"I do not pray for these alone, but also for those who will believe in Me through their word; that they all may be one, as You, Father, are in Me, and I in You; that they also may be one in Us, that the world may believe that You sent Me." —John 17:20–21

The overwhelming outpouring of love for humanity reflected in Jesus' prayer in Gethsemane should humble us and compel us to consider our response each day.

Jesus Is Arrested

Judas came to the place where Jesus and His disciples had camped, leading a detachment of soldiers and some officials from the temple. Jesus was arrested and taken to the house of the high priest. Peter had followed from a distance and sat with some people around a fire. A servant girl recognized him as a follower of Jesus. "I don't know Him" was Peter's response. Later another person identified him, and again, Peter denied a relationship with Jesus. Finally a third person positively identified him; Peter was adamant: "Man, I don't know what you're talking about!"

As Peter made his third denial, the rooster crowed, and the Lord looked straight at him. Peter remembered Jesus' prediction just hours earlier, and he went outside and wept bitterly. Before judging Peter too harshly, we must remember that if he were to be identified that night, there was a good chance he would share in the fate of Jesus—and this was before the good-news events following the cross. Peter was not yet ready to die for Christ, but that would change, and the world would be different because of the change.

Jesus was questioned by the high priest and then sent to Pilate, the Roman governor of Jerusalem, who sought to release Jesus. The high priest insisted on Jesus' death, telling Pilate that Jesus had begun stirring up trouble in Galilee, at which point Pilate decided to send Jesus to Herod, whose jurisdiction included the area of Galilee. Herod questioned Jesus, but he received no response; he then turned to mocking and ridiculing Jesus, dressing Him in an elegant robe and finally sending Him back to Pilate.

Again, Pilate wished to release Jesus, and He questioned Him, "Are you the King of the Jews?" Pilate wanted to know what Jesus had done that would cause the high priest to demand His execution. Jesus' response to Pilate speaks to Christians to this very day:

> *Jesus answered, "My kingdom is not of this world. If My kingdom were of this world, My servants would fight, so that I should not be delivered to the Jews; but now My kingdom is not from here."* —John 18:36

In hopes of pacifying the high priest, Pilate had Jesus flogged, soldiers placed a crown of thorns on His head, and clothed Him in a purple robe. Pilate again attempted to release Jesus and learned that the charge the high priest had brought against Him, punishable by death, was that Jesus had claimed to be the Son of God. On hearing this, Pilate was afraid and turned to Jesus for answers. Jesus gave him no answer. "Don't You realize I have power either to free You or to crucify You?" Pilate demanded in frustration.

> *Jesus answered, "You could have no power at all against Me unless it had been given you from above. Therefore the one who delivered Me to you has the greater sin."* —John 19:11

In another attempt to save Jesus' life, Pilate called on a custom of releasing a prisoner during the Feast of the Passover, and he asked the crowd to choose between Jesus and Barabbas, a notorious prisoner who had murdered many people. Surprisingly, the crowd demanded that Barabbas be released; Pilate continued to seek mercy for Jesus.

> *Pilate said to them, "What then shall I do with Jesus who is called Christ?" They all said to him, "Let Him be crucified!" Then the governor said, "Why, what evil has He done?" But they cried out all the more, saying, "Let Him be crucified!" When Pilate saw that he could not prevail at all, but rather that a tumult was rising, he took water and washed his hands before the*

multitude, saying, "I am innocent of the blood of this just Person. You see to it." And all the people answered and said, "His blood be on us and on our children." —Matthew 27:22–25

Pilate released the murderer Barabbas and handed Jesus over to be crucified. Like the careful politician he was, Pilate did not want to upset the majority of the public, even when he knew they were wrong. He did so even after his own wife warned him to have nothing to do with this innocent Man, as she had suffered a great deal that very day due to a dream she had had of Jesus' innocence. Though Pilate made a halfhearted effort to free Jesus on several occasions, he ultimately gave in and allowed an innocent man to be sentenced to a horrific death.

The Crucifixion

The time had come for Jesus to fulfill the prophecies found in the Old Testament, paying the ultimate price for man's sin and becoming the sacrificial Lamb of God.

Even while dying the cruel death on the cross, Jesus expressed His amazing love for us when He prayed, "Father, forgive them, for they do not know what they do"(Luke 23:34).

Jesus again expressed great love and His desire to save humanity when one of the criminals on the cross mocked Him, asking Him why He didn't just save Himself. The other criminal, however, rebuked the first, saying, "Don't you fear God?" And he asked Jesus to remember him when He came into His Kingdom. Jesus answered him:

Assuredly, I say to you, today you will be with Me in Paradise.
—Luke 23:43

From about noon until three in the afternoon that day, darkness covered the entire land. Jesus cried out in a loud voice, "My God, My God, why have You forsaken Me?" (Matthew 27:46), "Father, into Your hands I commit My spirit" (Luke 23:46), and finally, "It is finished," (John 19:30)—and He died. The Son of God, born of a virgin, who had never committed a sin, who prayed for all mankind at the Garden of Gethsemane, died on the cross. And at that very moment, the curtain of the temple was torn in two—from top to bottom (this was the entrance to the Holy of Holies, the most sacred area of the temple). The earth shook and the rocks split in two.

Joseph, from Arimathea, a member of the Jewish council who had not consented to Jesus' death sentence, asked Pilate for Jesus' body. Joseph took the body, wrapped it in clean linen cloths, and placed it in his very own, brand-new tomb.

The next day, the chief priests went to Pilate and informed him that Jesus had predicted His own resurrection after three days; their concern was that the disciples would steal Jesus' body in order to fake the resurrection. They requested that the tomb be sealed and secured until after the third day had passed. Pilate agreed to their request.

The Empty Tomb

In all four of the gospels (Matthew, Mark, Luke, and John), we read that very early on the first day of the week, Mary Magdalene, Peter, and others among the followers of Jesus came to the tomb where Jesus had been placed, only to find that the stone (which was massive and had been definitively sealed by the Romans) had been rolled away. Jesus was not in the tomb. He appeared to Mary Magdalene at the tomb and later to His disciples, including Thomas, who doubted and had to touch Jesus' wounds before he would believe that Jesus had risen from the dead. After Thomas expressed his belief in the risen Christ, Jesus told him:

Thomas, because you have seen Me, you have believed. Blessed are those who have not seen and yet have believed. —John 20:29

In the first chapter of Acts we read that Jesus continued to appear to the disciples and others for a period of forty days after His resurrection. The next question to consider is, how would believers respond to the persecution they would experience after Christ had left and returned to heaven?

What a joy to embrace a heritage that includes a risen Savior, the hope of the world!

4

The Believers Are Scattered

The future did not look good for the followers of Christ after His arrest and crucifixion. The disciple whom Jesus had referred to as a "rock upon which He would build His Church" had denied that he even knew Him (as Jesus had predicted). Judas Iscariot had betrayed Jesus for thirty pieces of silver, as was predicted 500 to 800 years earlier in Psalm 41:9 and in Zechariah 11:12–13, and then he hanged himself. Other disciples were in hiding. In short, Christianity suddenly had every opportunity to fail and fade away, but it didn't. Why didn't it?

To appreciate why the Christian Church did not die before it even began, one must have an understanding of the events that immediately followed the crucifixion. In the twenty-fourth chapter of Luke, we read of a special meeting that took place on the road to Emmaus. Beginning with verse 30, Luke described the journey of two men who were walking together discussing the events that had just occurred in Jerusalem.

As they talked, Jesus suddenly came up and walked with them, but they were kept from recognizing Him. He asked them about the things they were discussing. The two men were amazed that this stranger had no knowledge of Jesus of Nazareth, whom they described as a prophet, the One they had hoped would redeem the people of Israel. Instead He had been handed over to the chief priests and crucified, but strangely His tomb was now empty, and some women were telling stories of a vision of angels.

Jesus answered them with a history lesson:

> *Then He said to them, "O foolish ones, and slow of heart to believe in all that the prophets have spoken! Ought not the Christ to have suffered these things and to enter into His glory?" And beginning at Moses and all the Prophets, He expounded to them in all the Scriptures the things concerning Himself.* —Luke 24:25–27

Jesus later opened their eyes so that they could recognize Him, then Jesus suddenly disappeared. Imagine receiving a history lesson from the risen Christ, then having your eyes opened to the connection between Old Testament prophecy and His recent crucifixion. After Jesus left the two men, they asked each other, "Did not our heart burn within us while He talked with us on the road, and while He opened the Scriptures to us?" (Luke 24:32).

I believe it is both significant and relevant that Jesus was giving a history lesson to these two men before He appeared to the eleven disciples. Part of the reason that the Church did not die out at this time was that Jesus continued to teach and show His great love for His believers even after His execution on the cross.

The Great Commission

Matthew recorded the instructions Jesus left the eleven disciples in Galilee—instructions that Christians strive to follow to this very day. They are best known as The Great Commission:

> *"All authority has been given to Me in heaven and on earth. Go therefore and make disciples of all the nations, baptizing them in the name of the Father and of the Son and of the Holy Spirit, teaching them to observe all things that I have commanded you; and lo, I am with you always, even to the end of the age."* —Matthew 28:18–20

Jesus appeared to an estimated five hundred people during the forty-day period between His resurrection and His ascension into heaven. He also warned the disciples not to leave Jerusalem at that time, but they were to wait for the gift that the Father had promised to them.

The book of the Acts of the Apostles, written by Luke, a companion of Paul who was generally believed to be a physician, records the events of the early Church. In the first chapter of Acts, we learn about the forty days that Jesus spent on earth after His resurrection, as well as the choosing of a replacement for Judas. They chose Matthias by the use of lots directed by the Holy Spirit.

The Day of Pentecost

The Day of Pentecost is an event in history of which I must profess ignorance as to its importance and its link to the Old Testament. I was aware of how a violent wind came from heaven and tongues of fire came to rest on each of the disciples (likely on all of those gathered with the apostles); they were filled with the Holy Spirit and they began to speak in foreign tongues—other languages. My ignorance relates to any prior knowledge of the Festival of Weeks, the Feast of the Harvest, and the Day of Firstfruits before this event in the New Testament. The aforementioned events all occurred on the same day: fifty days after the Sabbath of Passover Week, and they were described in the Law of Moses, the Pentateuch. Jesus continued to fulfill the law even seven weeks after His resurrection.

As those filled with the Holy Spirit began to speak in other languages, a crowd had formed. Many people in this crowd were foreign, and the people began to wonder how men from Galilee could speak to them in their own language—including Mesopotamians, Egyptians, Romans, and Arabs. Some people mocked them, proposing that they had drunk too much wine.

Three Thousand Are Baptized

Peter stood up and addressed the crowd, which was still in town for the Passover; the same Peter who had rejected Jesus earlier was now filled with confidence and conviction, and he gave the crowd an extensive history lesson. In addressing the large crowd, Peter quoted the Old Testament prophet Joel regarding the last days. Peter then made the connection with Jesus of Nazareth: that God had promised to place a descendant of King David on His throne. Peter told the crowd:

Therefore let all the house of Israel know assuredly that God has made this Jesus, whom you crucified, both Lord and Christ." —Acts 2:36

The people in the crowd were cut to their hearts, and they asked Peter, "What should we do?" His response was to "repent and be baptized." Peter pleaded with the crowd to save themselves from "this corrupt generation." About three thousand people accepted Christ that day and were added to the body of believers.

The First Christian Church

In today's modern age in which thousands of denominations thrive, it is difficult to imagine how the first Christian Church might have worked. It was only about fifty days after Christ's crucifixion and resurrection, and His appearance to many in Jerusalem; what kind of Church were the first Christians a part of? How did they worship? What about the temple? Most of us are familiar with some form of church service, and we know what we like and what we don't like. But Luke describes some of the characteristics of the first Church in the book of Acts:

> *And they continued steadfastly in the apostles' doctrine and fellowship, in the breaking of bread, and in prayers. Then fear came upon every soul, and many wonders and signs were done through the apostles. Now all who believed were together, and had all things in common, and sold their possessions and goods, and divided them among all, as anyone had need.*
> *So continuing daily with one accord in the temple, and breaking bread from house to house, they ate their food with gladness and simplicity of heart, praising God and having favor with all the people. And the Lord added to the church daily those who were being saved.*
> —Acts 2:42–47

People brought the sick into the streets to be healed by the apostles, which caused the high priest and the members of the Sadducees to become jealous. They had the apostles arrested and placed in the public jail. The account of their arrest is recorded in the fifth chapter of Acts, where we read that during the night an angel of the Lord opened the doors of their jail and instructed them to go stand in the courtyard of the temple and speak forth the message of the gospel. The next day the leaders of the temple sent for the apostles and found that the jail was secure—but empty! They were puzzled as to what had happened. When they learned that the apostles were in the temple courtyard instead of the jail, they brought them before the Sanhedrin—the full assembly of the elders of Israel—for questioning by the high priest.

> *Did we not strictly command you not to teach in this name? And look, you have filled Jerusalem with your doctrine, and intend to bring this Man's blood on us!* —Act 5:28

Peter responded by stating that the disciples must obey God rather than men, and he gave the Sanhedrin another brief history lesson, which greatly angered them. But one Pharisee named Gamaliel, a respected teacher, asked the apostles to leave the room as he addressed the Sanhedrin. Gamaliel gave them his own history lesson regarding disruptive men from past years, whose plans to destroy the peace had eventually failed. He then gave them this advice:

And now I say to you, keep away from these men and let them alone; for if this plan or this work is of men, it will come to nothing; but if it is of God, you cannot overthrow it—lest you even be found to fight against God."
—Acts 5:38–39

Gamaliel was said to be the most famous Jewish teacher of his time; the apostle Paul was actually one of his students. His words are indeed very wise, and they remind me of the words of another Pharisee named Nicodemus, the one who had visited Jesus one evening (see John 3:1–21). The Sanhedrin was persuaded by Gamaliel's speech, and they released the apostles after having them flogged, and they warned them not to speak in the name of Jesus again. The apostles left rejoicing, and they continued proclaiming the good news about Jesus in the temple courts, day after day.

This first Church, or fellowship of believers, grew quickly because those early believers were willing to put *everything* on the line. They were willing to go to prison, or even to die, for their faith; they would not be stopped by men. Gamaliel spoke wisely to his fellow elders when he said, "If it is from God, you will not be able to stop these men." We can see, over the next two thousand years how true his words would prove to be. A great deal of credit should be given to Gamaliel—his wise words spared the apostles a death sentence at that time, and they should speak to us even today.

Stephen, the First Martyr

The Church was continuing to grow, and men of faith were being asked to step up and lead, including a man named Stephen. Subsequently Stephen was falsely accused of blasphemy against Moses and brought before the Sanhedrin. His response provides us with an amazing summary of the history of Israel, dating back to Abraham, including Moses and the

Exodus, David, and the prophets. The seventh chapter of the book of Acts records Stephen's response to the charges of blasphemy made against him, in which he, like the apostles before him, accused the Jewish leaders of murdering the Righteous One. He pointed out that Moses had actually spoken about the coming of Christ (see Deuteronomy 18:15, 18).

Upon hearing Stephen's words, the members of the Sanhedrin became furious and dragged Stephen out of the city and began to stone him. Like Jesus, Stephen asked the Lord to not hold this sin against them before he "falls asleep" (died). A man named Saul was standing there at the execution, giving his approval to Stephen's death. On that day, a great persecution broke out against the Church in Jerusalem, and all of the believers, except for the first apostles, were scattered.

The Believers Were Scattered

Saul began a systematic search-and-destroy mission, and he personally began to arrest and imprison the believers he encountered in Jerusalem. Believers fled Jerusalem, but they still continued to preach the Word wherever they went (see Acts 3:4–5). Saul was a member of the Sanhedrin, a Pharisee, and a devout believer in the Jewish faith; he was convinced that the followers of Jesus were a dire threat to the Jewish faith. To accomplish his all-consuming goal of destroying the threat of the Christian Church, Saul asked for letters from the high priest to each of the synagogues in Damascus, giving him the authority to arrest any followers of "the Way" (the Christian sect).

Damascus was important to Saul because at the time it was the hub of commercial trade, where Syria, Mesopotamia, Arabia, and Persia converged. If Christianity grew in Damascus, it would quickly spread into other parts of the world, and Saul was determined to prevent that at any cost. While on the road to Damascus one day, however, Saul had an encounter with Jesus Christ Himself that changed his life. The encounter turned Saul from a threat to the Christian Church to a man who would be credited with the authorship of more books in the Bible than any other writer. He also taught at the Church in Antioch, where disciples were first called "Christians." In his initial encounter with Jesus on the road to Damascus, Saul was temporarily blinded and had to be led to Ananias, who was directed by Christ to take care of Saul.

It is important to understand Saul's level of education; his understanding of the books of the Old Testament cannot be questioned, nor can his commitment to them. Saul was also a citizen of Rome, which gave him both authority and special protection. Had he not encountered Christ while on his journey to Damascus, there is little doubt that he would have inflicted great pain on the believers there, but that was not God's plan. Saul's blindness ended after three days, and he then began to preach in the synagogues of Damascus.

People were both astonished and baffled. They knew that Saul had been coming to take Christians as prisoners, yet here he was, suddenly preaching the good news of Jesus. Later Saul tried to join up with the disciples in Jerusalem, but understandably, they were afraid of him; Barnabas, one of the disciples there, intervened on Saul's behalf, however, and Saul was accepted.

The original apostles, along with Matthias, who was chosen to replace Judas, and Saul (later called Paul) preached the news of Christ, and the Church grew throughout Judea, Galilee, and Samaria. The Christian Church continued to grow in the first century as Paul and the twelve disciples traveled on several missionary journeys, where all but John were eventually killed for their faith.

The Christian Church has been built on the blood of the risen Christ and the blood of the apostles, including Paul. The apostle John was eventually imprisoned on the island of Patmos, where he received a divine revelation about Christ. John was the only apostle who would die a natural death. Paul wrote thirteen (fourteen, if you include the book of Hebrews) letters to various churches and other disciples in order to educate and encourage them; these letters are now part of the twenty-seven books recognized as the New Testament.

The Price of Faith in the Early Church

By the end of the first century, thousands of believers have joined the Christian Church, but not without consequences such as risking arrest and death. Despite their threats, the Jewish leaders were unable to stop the growth of the Christian Church after the crucifixion and resurrection of Jesus as believers were willing to die for their faith.

The Catholic Church

It seems appropriate to mention that the beginning of the Christian Church was also the beginning of the Catholic Church. During the early years of the Church, there were no denominations, no splinter churches, nothing but one unified Church that faced severe persecution. My Protestant friends may be unfamiliar with the definition of the word "Catholic": it comes from the Greek *katholikos*, which is actually the combination of two words: *kata*—meaning "concerning," and *holos*—meaning "whole'; thus, *Catholic* means "concerning the whole." This word was first used by Saint Ignatius, the second bishop of Antioch after the apostle Peter, to refer to the Church. Remember, believers were first called "Christians" at Antioch. The Catholic Church would represent the united Christian Church for one thousand years—until the events of 1054, which are discussed later in this book.

Nero and Christian Persecution

By AD 64, Christianity had spread to Rome and had become popular among the poor and destitute people there. Believers spoke of a new kingdom and a new King, provoking suspicion among Roman authorities, who considered that way of thinking to be a threat to the Empire. In the summer of AD 64, Rome burned for six days, destroying almost three-quarters of the city. The people blamed Nero, thinking he did it for his own amusement. Nero laid the blame on Christians and arrested and tortured a few who, under torture, accused other believers.

Believers were rounded up and put to death in sadistic and horrible manners for the amusement of the citizens. They were nailed to crosses and set on fire to serve as evening lights. Thousands of Christians were killed under Nero's reign, including the Apostles Peter and Paul.

Polycarp

One of the most well-documented cases of early Church martyrdom was the death of Polycarp, the eighty-six-year-old bishop of Smyrna that occurred in AD 155. In *Foxe's Book of Martyrs*, John Foxe recorded Polycarp's arrest, during which he was asked, "What harm is it to say, 'Lord Caesar,' and to sacrifice and to save yourself?" But he would not do it; again he was told, "Consider thyself, and have pity on thy great age," and again he refused. Finally, before a great multitude and facing death by being burned alive, he again was urged by the proconsul, "Swear and I will release thee; reproach Christ."

> Eighty and six years have I served Him, and He never once wronged me; how then shall I blaspheme my King; who hath saved me?
> —*Polycarp*

At the age of eighty-six, Polycarp was burned alive at the stake for refusing to deny his Lord. This was a stunning display of courage and faith and should encourage all of us to stand firm in our belief in the Savior.

Despite the dire persecution, Christianity spread throughout the Roman Empire. In AD 197, Tertullian wrote, "There is no nation indeed which is not Christian." Again, *Foxe's Book of Martyrs* documents continued and severe Christian persecution under Roman Emperor Diocletian in the third century—referred to as the tenth persecution. From the time of the apostles until the time of Roman Emperor Constantine (AD 312), Christian persecution was intense—more for political reasons than religious ones. Unlike other religions that incorporated themselves with the other gods of the Roman pantheon, Christians would not give their primary allegiance to the Roman emperor and thus they were considered a threat to society.

The Jewish leaders were not able to rid the world of the Christian faith by requesting Pontius Pilate to execute Jesus on a cross. The arrest and/or death of each of the disciples did not wipe out Christianity. Severe persecution by no fewer than ten Roman emperors could not rid the world of Christianity. By the end of the first and second centuries, Christianity had spread into what is now Egypt, France, Italy, Greece, Great Britain, Libya, Tunisia, Morocco, Portugal, Austria, and other parts of North Africa.

Perpetua

Perpetua was a Christian noblewoman who, in AD 203, was one of the first five people martyred for her faith in Carthage (now Tunis) as part of an attempt to cripple Christianity in North Africa by the Emperor Septimius Severus. She was still breast-feeding her child when she was sentenced to death, and her pagan father begged her to renounce her faith so that she could be freed. "Father, do you see this vase here? Could it be called by any other name than what it is?" she asked him. "No," he answered. "Well, neither can I be called anything other than what I am, a Christian," she declared.

Moments before her execution, her father, holding Perpetua's infant son in his arms, pleaded with her, "Have pity on your baby!" The governor, Hilarianus, even tried to persuade her: "Have pity on your father's gray head; have pity on your infant son. Offer the sacrifice for the welfare of the emperor." "I will not," she replied. So she, and four others, were put to death.

This amazing act of bravery and courage occurred about 170 years after the resurrection of our Lord, Christ Jesus. Perpetua would rather leave her infant child behind than renounce her faith in Christ. I am very proud that she is part of my Christian lineage.

Cyprian

In AD 251, Cyprian, the bishop of Carthage, called a council to address divisions that were beginning to emerge within the Church. Some divisions were the result of people who had succumbed to the extreme pressure and persecution by the Romans and had said, "Caesar is Lord," but now they wanted to rejoin the Church body. Those who had not been tortured or survived the tortures would not allow easy admittance of the "lapsed." A priest named Novatus had started a church that offered easy admittance to these "lapsed" Christians. Cyprian was not happy with this division, and he desired to re-unify the Church at this council. For this purpose, he wrote *On the Unity of the Church*, in which he stated, among other things: "There is only one Church, of which the pope, in the person of Peter, is made the foundation; only those who are in His communion are in the Church." Cyprian's literary work contains several items that become significant in the future of the Catholic Church, as the acceptance of these ideas had the effect of increasing the power of the Church and the bishops.

In considering that the Church of the day had rejected the "lapsed," Peter's denial of Christ on the night before His crucifixion comes to mind. Peter would have been considered "lapsed" by the Church in AD 251, but our Lord Jesus Christ gave Peter a way back into the fold. Thank God that He forgives when man does not!

Canonization of the New Testament

As we discussed in the previous chapter, the Old Testament and the Apocrypha were translated into Greek during the third century BC and they were included in the Septuagint, which was widely used in the early Church. In describing the worship service of that time, Justin Martyr described the reading of the "memoirs of the apostles (the New Testament) or the writing of the prophets (the Old Testament)." The letters of the apostles were put into circulation during the second century, along with other writings that were ultimately not canonized, but it is unlikely that these books existed in a single volume.

On the Apologetics website toughquestionsanswered.org, post author Bill Pratt writes about the long and gradual process of the canonization of the New Testament, quoting Church historian J. N. D. Kelly from his book, *Early Christian Doctrines*:

> The main point to be observed is that the fixation of the finally agreed list of books, and of the order in which they were to be arranged, was the result of a very gradual process… Three features should be noted.
>
> First, the criterion which ultimately came to prevail was apostolicity. Unless a book could be shown to come from the pen of an apostle, or at least to have the authority of an apostle behind it, it was peremptorily rejected, however edifying or popular it might be.
>
> Secondly, there were certain books which hovered for a long time on the fringe of the canon, but in the end failed to secure admission to it, usually because they lacked this indisputable stamp…
>
> Thirdly, some of the books which were later included had to wait a considerable time before achieving universal recognition… By gradual stages, however, the Church both in the East and West arrived at a common mind as to its sacred books. The first official document which prescribes the twenty-seven books of our New Testament as alone canonical is Athanasius's Easter letter for the year 367, but the process was not everywhere complete until at least a century and a half later.

Mr. Pratt goes on to point out reasons we should want to know the true history of the canonization: "If you don't know what really happened, then you won't be able to recognize revisionist historians who grossly distort or outright lie about Christian origins." Pratt also quotes *The Da Vinci Code*, a popular book by author Dan Brown, which grossly misrepresented the process of canonization of the New Testament.

Despite the intense persecution, torture, and murder of early Christians, the faith grew throughout the world. The scholar Tertullian, who was converted after seeing the courage of the Christians who went to their deaths rather than forsake Christ, made the famous saying: "The blood of the martyrs is the seed of the church." Tertullian lived between AD 160 and AD 225, and he is also credited with coining the phrase "trinity" to describe the relationship between God the Father, God the Son, and God the Holy Spirit. Rome's horrific persecution of Christians would finally end under Constantine.

Even a basic understanding of history can protect us from the many misrepresentations and lies that date back through the ages. Heresy is nothing new; the enemy is patient and he is constantly seeking an opportunity to devour you. This is yet another reason *your history matters.*

5

Constantine

In AD 312, Diocletian was dead, and the position of emperor of Rome was opened up to two men, Constantine and Maxentius. They were to meet in battle to decide who would be emperor. Considered to be the "Father of Church History," Eusebius chronicled the history of Constantine, who is said to have seen, on the afternoon before his battle with Maxentius, a flaming cross across the sky accompanied by the Greek words: *"In this sign conquer."* Constantine also heard a voice commanding him to have his soldiers mark their shields with the symbol of Christ. After doing so, Constantine won the battle and became the emperor.

This victory is significant in Christian history because it represents the first time a Roman emperor would look favorably upon the Christian faith. In fact, Constantine's mother, Helena, was a Christian herself, and Christianity became the official faith of the Roman Empire at this time.

Under Constantine's rule, the Roman Empire was strengthened and Christianity flourished. The capital city of the Roman Empire was moved east and became known as New Rome, more commonly referred to as Constantinople. Constantinople was built with the worship of the Christian God as its foundation, rather than any pagan deities. By the end of the fourth century, it had become the largest and most culturally vibrant city in the Eastern Empire, and it would be the most important Christian city in the world for the next thousand years.

Eusebius, Bishop of Caesarea: "Father of Church History"

In AD 324, Eusebius completed the first surviving history of the Christian Church, which includes the period dating back to the time of the apostles. *Christian History,* or *Ecclesiastical History,* is a very important work because Eusebius had access to materials that are no longer available to us today. Because of his efforts, we still are able to learn details of the lives and deaths of the apostles and other significant people who made a difference in the development of the early Church.

The Council of Nicaea in AD 325: History versus *The Da Vinci Code*

Until recent years, I had not been familiar with the Council of Nicaea, nor was I familiar with the details of the bestselling book by Dan Brown *The Da Vinci Code*. Every Christian should have risen up in outrage over the false history of the Council of Nicaea as portrayed in Mr. Brown's fictional account of the event. In his book, Brown suggests that the divinity of the Lord Jesus Christ was actually debated and that Jesus had originally been viewed by His followers as a mortal prophet until the time of this council. Brown also suggested that Constantine assembled an entirely new Bible during the council; his own prejudices prompted him to choose only books that spoke of Jesus as divine. Of course, however, to be outraged at Brown's audacity, we would need to possess a working knowledge of the purpose and outcome of the Council of Nicaea.

One excellent account of the Council of Nicaea, including a comparison to the telling of the event in *The Da Vinci Code*, can be found at the website www.religionfacts.com/da_vinci_code/nicea.htm. The main purpose behind Constantine's calling together the Council of Nicaea was to address the issue raised by Arius, on whether Christ was actually a divine creation of the Father or was Himself co-eternal and equal with God. The vote by the bishops was not close. While the council did consider other issues, including the calendar date of Easter and questions of church organization, it did not question the canon of the Bible. In fact, the canonization of the New Testament had started centuries before Constantine's influence. The gospels of Matthew, Mark, Luke, and John had already been accepted nearly 150 years before.

Christians should look to the Jews with respect to the ways they have protected their history and taught their children not to forget it. Our own children are looking to us in the same way; if Christian history means nothing to us, it will mean nothing to them. History becoming myth and myth becoming history should be a real fear for true people of faith.

The Nicene Creed

During the Council of Nicaea (held in AD 325), the following statement of faith was adopted. Known as the Nicene Creed, it is still recited in churches today.

> We believe in God the Father almighty maker of all things, visible and invisible. And in one Lord Jesus Christ, the only-begotten of the Father, that is, begotten of the substance of the Father, God from God, light from light, true God from true God, begotten, not made, of the same made, in heaven and earth; who for us humans and our salvation came down, took flesh, and was made human, suffered and rose again on the third day, ascended into heaven, and will come to judge the living and the dead. And in the Holy Spirit.

With a Christian emperor on the throne and an end to the persecution, there were no more martyrs. The Church moved from meeting secretly in private homes, to meeting in buildings built in the style of houses (around AD 261), to meeting in more formal basilicas.

The Basilica

Under Constantine's rule, the Church began a lavish building program in the western portion of the Roman Empire. This building program spread into the eastern portion of the empire after Constantine was crowned emperor there, as well, in AD 324. The first church building of significance was the Basilica of Saint John Lateran, in Rome, which could seat about 3,000 people and was decorated with gold and marble. Much larger and even more influential was the Basilica of Saint Peter, which historians believe was begun by Constantine between AD 319 and 333, and was ultimately torn down and rebuilt in the sixteenth century to its present form. Saint Peter's Basilica can accommodate 60,000 worshipers, and it is considered the largest house of worship in the world. It is also the supposed site of the tomb of the apostle Peter, whom Roman Catholics consider to be the first pope.

Also under the rule of Constantine, Christianity was no longer a persecuted faith; the emperor strongly supported the Church and funded the construction of its new buildings. As the fourth century came to a close, the fruits of the labor of the early Church were evident. An end had come to the persecution of the Church, as the Roman Empire adopted Christianity (officially by Emperor Theodosius in AD 391). The books of the New Testament were officially recognized in AD 367 by the widely circulated Easter Letter, written by the highly Orthodox Bishop of Alexandria, Athanasius. The Council of Carthage in AD 397 finally confirmed the list of New Testament books.

Codex Sinaiticus: The World's Oldest Bible

Believed to have been written around AD 350, the Codex Sinaiticus is the oldest complete copy of the New Testament; it contains portions of the Septuagint Old Testament. Unfortunately, however, monks used pages from the Old Testament to light fires. This Codex was discovered in Saint Catherine's Monastery, which was founded in the sixth century and is considered to be the oldest Christian monastery in the world. In 1844 at Saint Catherine's in Egypt, the Codex Sinaiticus was located and is now considered to be one of the most important texts for studying ancient Greek translations of the New Testament. In 2002, a major international project was undertaken to create an electronic version of the Codex, which includes the history of the book, and in 2009 the electronic version of the Codex was made available online. Photos of the Codex, including an English translation, can be found at http://www.codex-sinaiticus.net/en.

The Vulgate

In AD 366, Damasus was the bishop of Rome. He wanted the Church to be free of the Greek influence of the Septuagint and become fully Latin. To accomplish this, he desired to have the Bible translated into Latin. Damasus's secretary was named Eusebius Hieronymus Sophronius, better known as Saint Jerome. Known as the Vulgate, Jerome's translation of the Old and New Testaments into Latin began in AD 382 and was completed in AD 405. The Vulgate became the official Bible of the Church for the next thousand years.

Jerome had begun the process of translating the Bible into Latin by working directly from the Septuagint, but he also decided to consult with Jewish scholars out of a desire to work directly from the Hebrew text, thinking it would result in a more accurate translation. Jerome's Vulgate includes seven books in the Old Testament and additions to the books of Esther and Daniel that were not part of the Hebrew text and are not included in Protestant Bibles today. These seven Old Testament books, which are part of the Apocrypha, include Tobit, Judith, 1 and 2 Maccabees, the Wisdom of Solomon, Ecclesiasticus (or Sirach), and Baruch.

The first-century historian Josephus referred to the Old Testament books of the Hebrew Bible in his book *Against Apion*. The twenty-two books he described were actually equivalent to the thirty-nine books recognized as canon in the King James Bible, as well as in other Bibles used by Protestants today. The following is an excerpt from *Against Apion* that relates to the books that Josephus believed were divinely inspired:

For we have not an innumerable multitude of books among us, disagreeing from and contradicting one another, [as the Greeks have,] but only twenty-two books, which contain the records of all the past times; which are justly believed to be divine; and of them five belong to Moses, which contain his laws and the traditions of the origin of mankind till his death. This interval of time was little short of three thousand years; but as to the time from the death of Moses till the reign of Artaxerxes king of Persia, who reigned after Xerxes, the prophets, who were after Moses, wrote down what was done in their times in thirteen books. The remaining four books contain hymns to God, and precepts for the conduct of human life. It is true, our history hath been written since Artaxerxes very particularly, but hath not been esteemed of the like authority with the former by our forefathers, because there hath not been an exact succession of prophets since that time; and how firmly we have given credit to these books of our own nation is evident by what we do; for during so many ages as have already passed, no one has been so bold as either to add anything to them, to take anything from them, or to make any change in them; but it is become natural to all Jews immediately, and from their very birth, to esteem these books to contain Divine doctrines, and to persist in them, and, if occasion be, willingly to die for them.

The apocryphal books were placed in between the Old Testament and New Testament in Jerome's translation and clearly noted that they were not canon, but were separate from the Holy Scriptures. However, later editions of the Vulgate recognized seven books of the Apocrypha as Scripture.

As the Church entered the fifth century, it had gained much ground in the world of that day. Believers were no longer meeting in secret in the Roman Empire; instead the Church had the full support of the government. Also bishops were gaining power among the people and with the government.

In studying the history of the Church, we have the benefit of considering both the Scriptures and the actual history of Rome, but we still need to remember the words of John and Paul as we move forward to study a period of growing power of the Church and bishops:

Do not love the world or the things in the world. If anyone loves the world, the love of the Father is not in him. For all that is in the world—the lust of the flesh, the lust of the eyes, and the pride of life—is not of the Father but is of the world. And the world is passing away, and the lust of it; but he who does the will of God abides forever. —1 John 2:15–17

And do not be conformed to this world, but be transformed by the renewing of your mind, that you may prove what is that good and acceptable and perfect will of God. —Romans 12:2

So, what will become of the Christian Church in this new age of acceptance in the Roman Empire? We learned in the previous chapter that after the time of Christ, the believers were scattered, persecuted, forced to meet in secret, and martyred for their beliefs. Despite these obstacles, the Church grew in unprecedented ways. Later, the basilica became the standard for houses of worship—supposedly a significant improvement over meeting in private homes. In the fourth century, the influence of Christianity began to experience growth both in power and in wealth that would continue for the next thousand years.

Under the reign of Constantine, the Church enjoyed state sponsorship and it expanded significantly. Larger buildings were needed to accommodate the increasing number of believers, so basilicas were constructed throughout the empire to allow for believers to meet together. With increasing church sizes, the role of bishops grew in importance, both in the Church and in society. In a large city, the bishop would be like the CEO of a large company, and he delegated most of the operations of the Church to other people.

The hierarchy of the bishops was formed during the fifth and sixth centuries, and by the sixth century, bishops of large cities were known as archbishops. Above the archbishops were the patriarchs. There is general agreement that the first three patriarchs were the bishops of Rome, Alexandria, and Antioch. A patriarch could claim authority over bishops of neighboring cities. For example, the bishop of Alexandria would have had authority over other Egyptian bishops, including Cyrenaica (Libya). The patriarch of Antioch would have had authority over the Eastern churches. And the patriarch of Rome would have had authority over Italy and the Western churches. The Church was becoming highly organized with magnificent basilicas reflecting breathtaking architecture.

While the Church was gaining power and influence, it was also helping the empire care for its poor, including the construction of houses (hostels) that assisted poor and hungry travelers. The price paid by the Church to be accepted by the state was steep, however; the emperor considered himself to be equal to a bishop, and as master of the empire, he also believed himself to be the master of the Church. The sons of Constantine had similar views regarding the relationship between the emperor and the Church.

Also during this time of the reign of Constantine, the belief of Arius that Christ was not actually divine, known as *Arianism*, had gained considerable prominence. In AD 381, the Council of Constantinople was called in opposition—to reaffirm that the Son and the Holy Ghost were officially divine in nature, just as the Father was.

In AD 394, Emperor Theodosius defeated a barbarian horde and reunited the empire. During this time he enacted legislation that outlawed paganism; Christianity thus had complete prominence in the Roman Empire and became the official religion of the state. Under Theodosius's reign, other faiths were outlawed and Christians began destroying the pagan temples.

The Byzantine Empire

Constantine eventually moved the capital seat of the Roman Empire eastward to the city of Byzantium, which was then finally referred to as "Constantinople" in AD 330. The city became the center of the Eastern Orthodox Church and accepted all people as long as they were prepared to accept the Orthodox religion. It was believed that Byzantium had been founded by the apostle Andrew, brother of the apostle Peter. This claim to fame placed the city on nearly equal footing with Rome, whose church had once been led by Peter. Constantinople became the home of the great cathedral *Hagia Sophia*, as well as about three hundred additional monasteries, and it was protected by large walls, which the inhabitants believed would protect them as long as they were faithful to the orthodoxy of the Church. Unfortunately this was not the case, and the city fell to the Muslims in 1453, when it became the capital seat of the Ottoman Empire, and the *Hagia Sophia* was transformed into a mosque. Today Constantinople is known as Istanbul, and the *Hagia Sophia* has been transformed into a museum.

Antony of Egypt

Considering how busy our lives are today in the twenty-first century, it is easy to imagine having a strong desire to get away from everything to spend time with God. Imagine for a moment what life must have been like in Rome; imagine being a new convert, someone who was hearing of the gospel of Jesus Christ for the very first time.

Antony was a man of wealth who lived in a rural area of Egypt. Upon hearing the gospel, he converted to Christianity. He took the message of Jesus very seriously, including selling all he had to give to the poor and living alone, first among tombs, and then in the middle of the desert. Antony wanted to be alone with God and live a quiet existence. Unfortunately, word of his wisdom and insights became widespread. People flocked to see him, and he taught them about Christ. It is interesting that during the time of Antony, a time when the Church was experiencing such great success and prominence, many people were not happy with their society. A growing feeling was spreading that the empire might be nearing its end. Thousands of people from several parts of the empire began to follow Antony's example and move to the desert.

From Antony's example, communities sprang up, in which people lived simple lifestyles that were devoted to God. In AD 320, a pagan soldier named Pachomius, who had converted to Christianity upon meeting some of the hermits living in the desert, became a hermit himself. He was joined by several people, and he decided to set up rules for their newly formed communities. By the time he died in AD 346, there were eleven communities in place who followed the teachings of Pachomius: two for women and nine for men. Pachomius was the instigator of the monastic movement, and these communities made up the first true monasteries, with these followers being the first Christian monks.

It is worth repeating here that in an era when people were no longer persecuted or martyred because of their faith, the Church was able to move out of people's homes and into beautiful basilicas, and Christianity had become accepted by the state, in the midst of all of this "acceptance," the monastic movement was born. People who were seeking a true and closer relationship with God were not finding it in the Church as early as the fourth century after Christ—perhaps due to its revered position in the empire.

The Fall of Rome

In AD 410, the city of Rome was invaded and sacked by Alaric the Visigoth and his barbarian hordes; this marked the first time Rome had been attacked in nearly eight centuries. Part of the reason for the weakness in Rome at this time was that, in the past, their conquered peoples had been incorporated into the Roman culture. "Romanization" meant that new, conquered lands and people became part of the existing culture; they were to leave their old culture behind. Throughout the late fourth century and during all of the fifth century, the western part of the Roman Empire effectively dissolved into a number of smaller barbarian kingdoms.

The fall of the western portion of the Roman Empire is considered to be the beginning of the Middle Ages by many historians. The eastern part of the empire, located in Constantinople, was able to continue after the fall of Rome for several hundred more years.

These are more bricks in the wall of an important heritage—our heritage.

6

Light Invades the Dark Ages

The period between the sixth and thirteenth centuries is sometimes referred to as the "Dark Ages" by historians. A close examination of our heritage reveals that the Light of the World, the Lord Jesus Christ, shone brightly even during the Dark Ages, and our Church family expanded. Because of my Irish heritage, I am particularly pleased to write about God's use of Patrick in Ireland.

Patrick Converts Ireland

Ireland was converted to Christianity through the efforts of Patrick around AD 432, including the establishment of about three hundred churches and the baptism of approximately 120,000 people. Even though Ireland was a pagan country before Patrick began his mission, it underwent a relatively peaceful conversion process, with no martyrs. People believed that Patrick was acting on behalf of God. Later, when new missionaries visited Ireland, they found a vibrant faith; the priests and monks were learned men, and the Church had a penetrating effect on the people. What is interesting about the Church in Ireland is that it actually developed outside of the Church of Rome, but around monasteries, which reflected the original tribal system of the country. There were no church bureaucracies; monks were encouraged to devote themselves to the activities of preaching, studying, and ministering to the poor. The Church of Ireland did not formally become part of the Catholic Church until much later, around the twelfth century.

Columba Evangelizes Scotland

In AD 563, an Irishman named Columba, along with twelve companions, sailed to Scotland, where they erected modest homes and a plank church to begin their missionary activities. Beginning with the chief of

Inverness, named Brude, Columba sought to convert key people to the gospel message. He traveled across Scotland and spread the gospel, successfully evangelizing the entire country. He also became the abbot of a large monastery on Iona. After Columba's death, evangelists from Iona spread out and created new monasteries in Europe. Each of these new monasteries looked to Iona for guidance. Despite various invasions from Vikings, Iona survived until the monastery was finally torn down during the time of the Reformation.

As my own background is Irish and Scotts-Irish, I was very interested to gain an understanding of how Ireland and Scotland came to be Christian nations in the fifth and sixth centuries. Saint Patrick and Saint Columba are buried at Down Cathedral, in County Down in the country of Ireland.

Pope Gregory I, "The Great"

Though Rome was no longer the capital of the empire, the city of Rome still had great importance to the Church, having had connections with both Peter and Paul. Bishops in Rome had been working to increase their power; the bishop of Rome was now considered the pope—the leader of the Church.

Gregory had been born to a noble family in AD 540, and he had been named the prefect of Rome, the highest civil office, before turning away from that lifestyle. He resigned his office and gave up his estates so that monasteries could be formed, and he even joined one himself, eventually becoming an abbot. In AD 590, he was asked to become the pope. Gifted with great administrative skills, he proved to be of great assistance to the emperor, although he had no true political ambitions.

Pope Gregory I was extremely concerned about pastoral care, and he desired for clergy to see themselves as shepherds and servants of their flocks. He authored the book *Pastoral Rule*, which became somewhat of a clergy textbook of the Middle Ages. He also wrote *Dialogues*, a book about the saints that emphasized the miraculous and made them seem bigger than life. While he was pope, the veneration of body parts, clothing, and the like of saints was encouraged. Gregory also believed in purgatory, was interested in church music, and sent missionaries to Great Britain, including sponsoring a mission to Kent under Augustine, who later became the first Archbishop of Canterbury. On Christmas Day in AD 597, the year when Augustine arrived in England, ten thousand people were baptized, including King Ethelbert of Kent. During the fourteen years of Gregory I's papacy, so much was achieved that he was later named "Gregory the Great."

The Rise of Islam

In approximately AD 610, a man named Muhammad in the Arabian Peninsula claimed to have received divine revelations, and he declared that he was a prophet of God. In AD 622 he fled his home in Mecca to the oasis in Medina, where he founded the first Muslim community. In AD 630 he launched a military assault and defeated his opponents in Mecca. By AD 632 the new religion of Islam had swept through Palestine and Syria and even conquered Jerusalem. By AD 640 Islam had invaded Egypt and North Africa and nearly eradicated Christianity in that region, which had once numbered over one million believers. The Dome of the Rock was completed around AD 691, constructed on the Temple Mount in Jerusalem. The site of the gold-domed shrine of Islam is of great importance to Jews and Christians as well as Muslims and is believed to be the most contested piece of real estate on earth.

Islam has had a significant impact on the world. For the most part, it is highly intolerant of Christianity, or any other religion, in the areas of the world they control, primarily Middle Eastern countries. By October 2013, there were approximately 1.3 billion adherents of the Islamic faith in the world, making them the second largest religion in the world in terms of individual followers. At two billion, the largest world religion is Christianity (when Catholics, Orthodox believers, and Protestants are combined in the total).

The expansion of the Islamic military was one of the most dangerous threats facing Christianity during the early eighth century. In AD 711, the Moorish forces invaded Spain, where Islam ruled the country until a revolt took place in AD 750. Because of this revolt, the Muslim forces were overthrown in the northwest part of Spain and the people reverted back to Christianity. It took seven more centuries before the rest of the people of Spain would be able to overthrow their Muslim leadership and return to Christianity.

The Venerable Bede:
Ecclesiastical History of England

As a great believer in the importance of preserving our Christian heritage for future generations, it encourages me to read about great minds like Bede, who spent a large portion of his life in a monastery in northern England—beginning around AD 642. Bede became a priest at the age of thirty and devoted the remaining years of his life to writing, including the composition of Bible commentaries and other related works. In *Historia Ecclesiastica Gentis Anglorum* (*Ecclesiastical History of England*), Bede recorded the history of England dating from Julius Caesar to his present day of AD 731. While the book contained history in general, its main focus was on how Christianity developed in England and ultimately replaced paganism.

Just as the Jewish scribes carefully preserved the history of their people, Bede's *Ecclesiastical History of England* preserved an important segment in the development of Christianity that might otherwise have been lost. From his book we can see how a diverse group of tribes became a single nation with one unifying religion.

The Book of Kells

Dating back to about AD 800, *The Book of Kells* is a beautifully illuminated manuscript that contains the four Gospels written in Latin. It is considered a national treasure of Ireland and "the finest surviving manuscript to have been produced in medieval Europe" (see About.com, "Medieval History"). *The Book of Kells* is fascinating because it is difficult to understand how the complex and intricate decorations were crafted by hand without the benefit of even a magnifying glass, which was not available at the time. The dating of *The Book of Kells* relates to the time of Viking raids in Iona, where it is believed work on the book occurred. After one such raid in the ninth century it is believed the book was moved to Kells, Ireland. It was stolen in the eleventh century, at which time its cover was removed and, unbelievably, thrown into a ditch. Although it suffered water damage, it is still remarkably well-preserved.

The book was relocated by the Catholic Church in 1541 for its own protection, but it was returned to Ireland in the seventeenth century. *The Book of Kells* was eventually given to Trinity College in Dublin, where it resides to this day.

Charlemagne

Charlemagne was known as the "Father of Europe," and crowned emperor of Rome in AD 800. Under Charlemagne's rule, Christians had what many present-day Christians desire: the combination of Church and state and a leadership that was entirely Christian, including the emperor. Since the time of Constantine, the Church had grown in power and influence, and now, if the emperor was also a Christian, who then would have the greatest authority? After taking the throne, Charlemagne would expand the empire, and within three decades a large part of Europe was under his control. He took his role as a Christian emperor very seriously and began all of his correspondence with the words "Charles, by the will of God, Roman Emperor."

The Carolingian Renaissance

Charlemagne was not a learned man himself, but he held learning in high esteem. Under his rule there was a resurgence of art and scholarship that became known as the Carolingian Renaissance. During this period, the emperor founded schools and decreed that every monastery should have a school for teaching "all those who with God's help are able to learn." The Carolingian Renaissance was responsible for the preservation of a great many writings from the ancient world as monks made copies in the monasteries.

Charlemagne can also be credited for bringing about a standardization of legal systems in Europe. He accomplished this by issuing a series of edicts, or "capitularies," designed to allow different ethnic groups to use their own laws when those laws were not in conflict with Roman law. Laws were enforced by *"missi dominici"* who worked in pairs and traveled throughout the empire to inspect local governments and systems of justice. Prior to this time in the empire, different people followed different traditions and laws, mostly unwritten.

> Everyone shall live entirely in accordance with God's commands, justly and under a just rule, and everyone shall be ordered to live in harmony with his colleagues in his job or profession.
> —*Capitulary of the Missi, Charlemagne AD 802*

While Christianity was spreading throughout the Western Empire and the Western Church regained its prominence, the Eastern Church declined. After Charlemagne died in AD 814, his empire began to weaken, after being split between his three grandsons in AD 843. In AD 846, Muslims sacked Rome.

Christianity in England

During the reign of Charlemagne, Egbert, king of the West Saxons, succeeded in making Wessex a powerful kingdom. Egbert was accepted as king in Essex, Kent, Surrey, and Sussex, and he is believed by many to be the first "king of England"—crowned in AD 829. Since the time of Saint Patrick in AD 420 through the time of Pope Gregory I in AD 590, Christianity in England had developed and grown. The monasteries established by Patrick had proven to be of great benefit to the Christian faith, as they provided centers for people dedicated to the faith to study, live, work, and pray.

Christianity Comes to Russia

In AD 863, brothers Cyril and Methodius, Christian missionaries among the Slavic people, were sent to Moravia at the request of Rostislav, the ruler, who had appealed to the emperor of Constantinople. The brothers soon became very familiar with the language of the region and began translating the Scriptures into Slavonic. They invented an alphabet that became the foundation of the Russian alphabet. At this point in history, the Church would not allow the Scriptures to be written in any language other than Greek or Latin. In later centuries, hundreds of people were martyred during the Reformation as people sought to have the Bible translated into their native languages. Amazingly, however, when Cyril and Methodius traveled to Rome to appeal to Pope Adrian II to sanction the translation and worship by the Moravians in their native tongue, the pope agreed.

Years later, around the year AD 988, when the prince of Russia, Vladimir Sviatoslavich the Great, sought a religion by which to unite the people of Russia, his choice was between Roman Christianity and the Eastern Orthodox Church centered in Constantinople. The prince sent out representatives to investigate each of the two faiths. The representatives were overwhelmed by the spirit after attending a service at the *Hagia Sophia*, the Church of Holy Wisdom in Constantinople, where they reported:

> We do not know whether we were in heaven or on earth, for surely there is no such splendor or beauty in heaven or on earth. We cannot describe it to you. Only we know that God dwells there among men and their service surpasses the worship of all other places. [This should be the prayer of every Christian Church...that God would dwell there!]

Vladimir chose Orthodoxy, he married the sister of the Byzantine emperor named Anna, and he was baptized. Because of Cyril and Methodius, people in Russia could now worship God in their own language, Slavonic, in beautiful churches built by Vladimir and by rulers who followed. During his life he wiped out paganism, established schools, and made Christianity the official religion of Russia. Before dying he gave all of his possessions to the poor.

Christianity Comes to the Vikings

I was familiar with Erik the Red and his son, Leif Erickson, and knew they were famous for discovering new lands, such as Greenland. I didn't know, however, that Leif had been introduced to, and accepted, Christ during one of his early trips to Norway. In AD 999 Leif, as well as all of his men, were baptized before leaving Norway and returning to Greenland. Upon his return, he taught his faith to the people of Greenland, including his mother, who was converted and asked her husband, Erik the Red—Leif's father—to construct a church. While he did agree to build it, he did not accept the faith of his wife and son.

While it is encouraging to write about the expansion of Christianity into England, Russia, and Greenland by the end of the first millennium, Islam was also growing in Egypt and in western North Africa, where Christianity had been all but wiped out.

Researching Christian heritage introduced me to Vladimir of Russia, his desire to bring Christianity to his country, and the reaction of his men to a very spiritual worship experience at the *Hagia Sophia* in Constantinople. Because of the experience at the *Hagia Sophia*, Orthodox

Christianity became the faith of Russia. In the second millennium, we see the Roman Catholic Church growing powerful in Western Europe and the Greek Orthodox Church, centered in Constantinople, becoming powerful in Eastern Europe. Imagine—if the two churches had united, the history of the world might have been different, but the churches of the East and West are not united. In fact, they are far from it.

The Great Schism of 1054:
The Orthodox Church Separates from Rome

In reading the history of the Roman Catholic Church and the Orthodox Church as a twenty-first-century Christian, I have been amazed at how God has blessed each of these great organizations and used them to spread His Word throughout Europe, England, and Russia. Unfortunately, as is the case with many churches, at some point division—driven by pride, a desire for power, and other unChristlike characteristics—causes disruption. When church leadership cannot agree on issues, the result is frequently a split. In the case of the Church of Rome and the Church of Constantinople, the first great Church split took place in 1054.

The Great Schism involved two great leaders of that day: Pope Leo IX of Rome and Michael Cerularius, the patriarch of Constantinople. The Church of Rome considered its bishop to be the highest authority in the Church, which would put him above the patriarch of Constantinople. Pope Leo desired the church in Constantinople to submit to him. There were also other differences between the Church of Rome and the Orthodox Church: Rome used the Latin Vulgate, did not allow priests to marry, and had a different style of worship from the Orthodox Church, which used the Greek text, allowed the priests to marry, but most importantly, did not recognize that any one bishop was infallible or entrusted with greater authority than other bishops. In the Roman Catholic Church, the pope would become the highest authority and could be judged by no one. A few years later, Pope Gregory VII would put in writing that the Roman Church had never erred and never would until the end of time.

The single event in history identified as marking the beginning of the schism took place in the summer of 1054, when Cardinal Humbert, the personal representative of Pope Leo, walked into a service at the *Hagia Sophia* in Constantinople and placed a Bull of Excommunication onto the altar, then walked out. Can you imagine being in a church that sixty-five years earlier had inspired representatives of Prince Vladimir himself to adopt the Orthodox faith, but then having a personal representative of the pope declare that the church wasn't even Christian? Each church would excommunicate the other in the end, effectively stating that the other was not a true Christian church.

There is some good news regarding the possible rejoining of the Catholic and Orthodox Church in our modern era. In 1965, the leaders of the two churches lifted the excommunication status of each other. And in November 2013, Pope Francis sent the following greeting to the Archbishop of Constantinople:

> Your Holiness, beloved brother in Christ, this is the first time that I address you on the occasion of the feast of the Apostle Andrew, the first-called. I take this opportunity to assure you of my intention to pursue fraternal relations between the Church of Rome and the Ecumenical Patriarchate.

I find the efforts to bridge this one-thousand-plus-year-old schism to be encouraging—not because I am Catholic or Orthodox, because I am neither, but because of the prayer of our Lord Jesus Christ in the Garden of Gethsemane on the night He was arrested:

> *I do not pray for these alone, but also for those who will believe in Me through their word; that they all may be one, as You, Father, are in Me, and I in You; that they also may be one in Us, that the world may believe that You sent Me."* —John 17:20–21

The Great Schism marked the first great division in the Church, but it would not be the last. In the twelfth century Nicetas, Archbishop of Nicomedia, wrote the following regarding the differences between the Eastern Orthodox Church and the Roman Catholic Church:

> My dearest brother, we do not deny to the Roman Church the primacy amongst the five sister Patriarchates; and we recognize her right to the most honourable seat at an Ecumenical Council. But she has separated herself from us by her own deeds, when through pride she

assumed a monarchy which does not belong to her office... How shall we accept decrees from her that have been issued without consulting us and even without our knowledge? If the Roman Pontiff, seated on the lofty throne of his glory wishes to thunder at us and, so to speak, hurl his mandates at us from on high, and if he wishes to judge us and even to rule us and our Churches, not by taking counsel with us but at his own arbitrary pleasure, what kind of brotherhood, or even what kind of parenthood can this be? We should be the slaves, not the sons, of such a Church, and the Roman See [the Roman See is the office of the supreme head of the Church] would not be the pious mother of sons but a hard and imperious mistress of slave.

Another difference between the churches of the East and West is the methodology used on the mission field. Where the Western Church would insist on use of the Latin liturgy by all converts, the Eastern Church adopts a liturgy in the vernacular of the converts, as seen in the translation of the Scriptures and the development of a Slavonic alphabet, which eventually led to the expansion of the Orthodox faith in Russia under Prince Vladimir.

The history of the Christian Church would be incomplete without an understanding of the Orthodox Church from the time of its split from the Roman Catholic Church in 1054. The Orthodox Church faced great challenges due to the growth of Islam in the Middle East; eventually Constantinople would fall to the Muslim armies. Indeed, the Roman Catholic Church was also confronted by the growth of Islam, but it raised an army to meet the challenge.

There has been great criticism of the Crusades raised in the last several years, but what is the true history of these battles? Like every other issue that involves history, most people have no idea what exactly the truth is about the events in question. I grew up singing "Onward Christian Soldiers" during Vacation Bible School, and I believe in putting on the "full armor of God" (as any good soldier would)—as described in Ephesians 6:10–12. Still, I had little knowledge of the actual events surrounding the Christian Crusades that occurred between 1095 and 1272 before I began researching this book. Why were the Crusades necessary? Did any good come from them?

Before answering these two questions, we need a basic understanding of the growth of Islam from its founding in AD 610 up to the time of the first Crusade launched in 1095. The word *"Islam"* means "total submission to God's (Allah's) will," and, like the followers of Christianity, followers of Islam believe theirs is the only true religion and the only path to salvation. A primary desire of the Islamic people has always been to unite the world under the banner of Islam, and from the mid-seventh century until the latter half of the eighth century, their armies were dominant, as Palestine, Iraq, Syria, Egypt, most of Persia, Spain, and the entire northern coast of Africa fell to them and were converted to Islam by the sword.

By the eleventh century Muslims had conquered most of the old Roman Empire. Islamic forces might possibly have overtaken Europe if not for their defeat in AD 732 in the Battle of Poitiers, which resulted in their permanent retreat from France. Christians living in conquered regions were ordered to dress in black and to hang wooden crosses from their necks. Word of this persecution of Christians under al-Hakim's rule reached the ears of Christians in the West and fueled a strong hatred of the Muslims, especially among Christian clergy. Finally, in the eleventh century, Pope Urban II issued a call to arms.

The Crusades: *"Deus Vult!"*

On November 27, 1095, Pope Urban II called on all Christians to unite in order to defend and protect Christian pilgrims during a speech at the Council of Clermont, promising assurance of salvation to anyone who died in the Crusade. Europe was listening, and those who heard shouted *"Deus vult!"* ("God wills it!"). All the participants knew was that they were to meet in Constantinople, and the emperor had no idea of the magnitude of the army that would arrive to help, which eventually totaled fifty thousand men. The first Crusade lasted about four years and resulted in the temporary reclamation of Jerusalem, as well as the establishment of several military organizations, including the Knights of the Temple (Templars) and the Knights of the Hospital of Saint John (Hospitallers—still known today as the Order of Malta and Saint John's Ambulance). There were three other major Crusades sponsored by the papacy; other individuals sponsored later Crusades. Beginning in 1095 and continuing through 1250, seven major Crusades ultimately were not successful in defeating Muslim (Moorish) expansion, with the exception of Spain—where the last of the Moorish power ended in 1492.

Saint Francis of Assisi

Now as He was going out on the road, one came running, knelt before Him, and asked Him, "Good Teacher, what shall I do that I may inherit eternal life?"

So Jesus said to him, "Why do you call Me good? No one is good but One, that is, God. You know the commandments: 'Do not commit adultery,' 'Do not murder,' 'Do not steal,' 'Do not bear false witness,' 'Do not defraud,' 'Honor your father and your mother.'"

And he answered and said to Him, "Teacher, all these things I have kept from my youth."

Then Jesus, looking at him, loved him, and said to him, "One thing you lack: Go your way, sell whatever you have and give to the poor, and you will have treasure in heaven; and come, take up the cross, and follow Me."

But he was sad at this word, and went away sorrowful, for he had great possessions. —Mark 10:17–22

Many people are familiar with Jesus' response to the rich young ruler, who desired to follow Him but was unable to do so because he was unwilling to sell his possessions. Few of us could give up everything for Christ (not that all of us should, but in the case of the rich young ruler, possessions had become a hindrance to his spiritual life). A few verses later, one of the disciples asked, "Who then can be saved?" (verse 26), to which Jesus responded, "With God all things are possible" (verse 27). The story of Francis Bernardone, the son of a wealthy cloth merchant in Assisi, Italy, is one that should inspire all of us, as he was able to do what the rich young ruler could not: give up his personal wealth.

Assisi was at war with a nearby city. Francis, dressed in knight's armor, lance, and plumed helmet, rode to battle but was captured and held as a prisoner of war for a year. His experiences as a prisoner of war caused him to question the value of wealth, and he was later moved to great compassion for a leper, whom he felt had the face of Christ. In 1206 he renounced his father's inheritance, resulting in his father's disowning him, and he dedicated himself to a life of poverty. In deserted chapels in nearby Assisi, Francis preached a simple message of love and service, generating a following of those willing to renounce their wealth. He drafted rules for the Franciscan Order and went to Rome to receive approval from the pope.

People responded to Francis, and his followers numbered in excess of three thousand by 1218. The Church had grown incredibly wealthy during this time, while the poor were left to starve, and the Franciscan Order brought attention to this condition of the day. Even those who could not make the sacrifice to join Francis supported his ministry. He participated in the fifth Crusade, going with the crusaders to Egypt, where he appeared and preached to the sultan. Francis died in October of 1226 and was canonized in 1228. His last words were, "I have done my duty; may Christ now teach you yours." Also of note is that Francis penned the words to one of my favorite hymns when he wrote "The Canticle of the Sun," known today as "All Creatures of Our God and King."

The late songwriter Rich Mullins, famous for penning "Our God Is an Awesome God" among other hits, was a follower of the practices of Saint Francis of Assisi and no doubt earned significant money from sales of his music. Yet he instructed his accountant to pay him only the amount of money earned by the average worker during the last years of his life. Any excess funds available were to be distributed to other ministries. While I don't believe Jesus taught that having wealth was in and of itself a sin, it is clear that the pursuit of wealth can be a great obstacle to the Christian lifestyle.

The Fourth Lateran Council of 1215

Knowledge of past events can serve as a light in the darkness, just as the Word of God is a "lamp unto our feet, and a light unto our path." The Catholic doctrine of transubstantiation, the belief that the bread and wine used during the communion service becomes the actual flesh and blood of Christ once consumed, was officially adopted during this three-day council. In addition Pope Innocent III desired for the papacy to control affairs of state as well as the Church, and he proclaimed that the pope was the representative of Christ on earth, as opposed to the representative of Peter, as was the case in the past. The council also set up rules whereby disagreement with the Church could be punished, including with the power to confiscate property, paving the way for the Papal Inquisition instituted in 1231.

A Lost Mission Opportunity

Because of Marco Polo, Kublai Khan, the leader of the Mongols, was interested in Christianity, and in 1266 he requested Pope Gregory X to send one hundred Christian teachers to baptize him and to teach his people. The pope, who was able to raise an army of tens of thousands to fight in the Crusades, sent only a few; this might possibly have been the greatest lost missionary opportunity of all time. If the one hundred Christian monks had been sent, Asia might be Christian today.

The Norman Conquest

The origins of the Normans can be traced back to the beginning of the tenth century, when the King of France gave a piece of land to a Viking chief named Rolio in hopes that the gift would prevent them from attacking France. Over time the land became known as Northmannia, and then Normandy. The Vikings intermarried with the French and by 1000, the Viking pagans had become French-speaking Christians. The Normans were known for their culture, musical traditions, military achievements, and innovations. Many Normans of France and Britain served in the Crusades.

Prior to 1066, the Normans had a great deal of contact with England, including Viking raids of the English coasts and occupation of several important ports. Over time there were conflicts between the Norman leaders and those of Saxon and areas of England. In 1066, the Normans, led by Duke William II, conquered England at the Battle of Hastings and killed the English king.

Many positive changes occurred in England as a result of the Norman Conquest, including the construction of churches and castles, improvements to the legal system, and most importantly, the development of an enlarged vocabulary with a simple grammar. Much of the foundation laid by the Normans exists to this day in the architecture and language of England.

Consider the Christian world as it existed in the twelfth and thirteenth centuries. Christianity was growing in England and other parts of Europe. After a thousand-year presence in the Roman Empire, Christianity was losing ground to Islam in Middle Eastern countries, Africa, and Asia. The Church has grown powerful, led by powerful popes who believed themselves to be the representatives of God on earth and who took great steps to ensure that heretics were eliminated. (Later we will discuss the period of the Inquisition.) Great churches were constructed, including Saint Peter's Basilica in Rome and the *Hagia Sophia* in Constantinople. Despite the power and wealth of the Church, men like Saint Francis of Assisi and others were called to live a simple life.

The Magna Carta

Believed to be one of the most important documents in English history, the Magna Carta set legal precedents that would be followed in England and areas of English expansion, including the United States, to this very day. In the early thirteenth century, King John of England was not succeeding in various wars abroad and he was taxing the barons in order to raise more funds for the conflicts. The barons did not support King John and they rebelled. The barons captured London, but they did not defeat the king's forces entirely. The king was forced to sit down with them in the spring of 1215, resulting in a compromise: the Magna Carta. The Magna Carta proclaimed certain rights of English subjects, including protection abroad, the rights of the Church, and the understanding that the king, barons, lords, citizens, and vassals were all equally subject to the rule of law. The sixty-third article deals with the freedom of the Church in England.

Early in the fourteenth century, one of the greatest epic poems of all time was written: Dante's *The Divine Comedy*. Dating back to 1321, *The Divine Comedy* tells the story of a man's pilgrimage through hell, purgatory, and heaven—from sin to salvation. The success of the poem may be attributed to the fact that Dante wrote about issues that he wrestled with in life that concern most people: the purpose of life, whether an afterlife exists, and the reason for an individual's existence. Dante's work influenced other great writers who followed, including Geoffrey Chaucer, John Milton, and James Joyce, to name a few.

The Black Death

Beginning in the mid-fourteenth century, the Bubonic Plague, also known as the Black Death, swept through Europe. Beginning in 1348, the Black Death was responsible for between seventy-five to two hundred *million* deaths over a three-year period. Most experts believe the plague was carried by fleas that lived primarily on rats and other rodents, but this was unknown at the time and not suspected until later. Suspected causes of the plague at the time varied, but they included suspicions that Jews were poisoning the water, which resulted in many Jews being expelled or even killed. Some Jews confessed under torture. In Strasburg, Germany, the entire Jewish population was given a choice to convert to Christianity or be executed; about two thousand were killed. Others believed the plague was a punishment from God for the sins of the people.

During this period, much of society broke down, and as the population was reduced, the influence of the Catholic Church also diminished, with many people questioning their faith; this created the seeds that led to Protestantism. In Siena, Italy, work stopped on the Siena Cathedral, the Duomo. If completed, the Duomo would have been the largest cathedral in the world, but the plague wiped out most of the population and the construction was never completed. Today, the unfinished nave is considered by many to be a lesson to Christians that we are all members of an unfinished Church awaiting the One who will finish it. Some byproducts of the Black Death include a greater emphasis on clinical medicine, growth in higher education, and the development of the scientific method.

The Hundred Years War

From 1337 to 1453, the kingdom of England and the kingdom of France were involved in a series of conflicts known as the Hundred Years War. The root of the conflict can be traced back to William the Conqueror, who ruled England in 1066 while at the same time retaining possession of the Duchy of Normandy in France. As owners of property in France, the English kings were required to pay homage to the king of France, but in 1337 Edward III refused to pay homage to Philip VI of France. This resulted in the confiscation of the property held by Edward III by Philip VI; Edward, in turn, declared that he, not Philip, was the rightful king of France.

The Hundred Years War holds significance for several reasons, including its giving rise to a sense of nationalism in both countries, improvements in military science, and the establishment of the first standing army in Western Europe since the time of the Roman Empire. There is also one figure who played a prominent role in the war in an unexpected way.

Joan of Arc

Joan of Arc was visited by God at the age of twelve, and she left home at the age of sixteen to answer her calling. She heard voices that told her she was to aid the future king in reclaiming France from the English invaders. Joan led the French forces to victory at the Battles of Orleans and Patay; Orleans is believed to be one of the turning points in the war. Joan was captured and sold to the English, where she was tried for heresy in the spring of 1431. Joan was burned at the stake on May 30, 1431, at the age of nineteen; her last words were "Jesus, Jesus, Jesus." Pope Callixtus III overturned her conviction about twenty-five years later.

Joan of Arc believed that she was an instrument of God, and she faced her battles fearlessly, including fighting while wounded. Her life is an important part of our Christian history, and she should be an inspiration to us all.

In closing this chapter, it is appropriate to quote G.K. Chesterton from his book, *Orthodoxy,*

> The Christian Church was the last life of the old society and was also the first life of the new. She took the people who were forgetting how to make an arch and she taught them to invent the Gothic arch. In a word, the most absurd thing that could be said of the Church is the thing we have all heard said of it. How can we say the Church wishes to bring us back to the dark ages? The Church was the only thing that ever brought us out of them.

7

The Reformation

The Morning Star of the Reformation

Though the actual Reformation wouldn't begin until the sixteenth century, the man credited with being the "Morning Star" of the Reformation, John Wycliffe, was born in 1330. His courage to stand up to the Catholic Church and act on his convictions inspired John Hus and others to do the same.

John Wycliffe studied mathematics, natural science, and theology at Oxford University, a school that dates back to 1096 in some form or another. Oxford's website mentions him in its historical records. He was an excellent student who received his doctorate in theology in 1372. Wycliffe believed the Church of his day had grown too wealthy, that money was being wasted, and that the Church of the 1300 should become more like the first-century Church.

Wycliffe taught that the only authority should be Scripture and he urged all men, "great and small, learned and unlearned," to acquaint themselves with God's law by reading the Bible for themselves. It was his desire to see God's Word made available to everyone—in the vernacular. Unfortunately, the only access common people had to God's Word was through the local priests, who were reading the Latin Vulgate. The Church did not agree with Wycliffe on the matter of making the Bible available in the English language to the average person.

Wycliffe rejected the Catholic doctrine of transubstantiation as well as individual confession, believing there was no biblical basis for the practice, and he repudiated indulgences (the selling of forgiveness) and the selling of indulgences (the forgiveness of sin). Wycliffe's convictions caused great tension between himself and the Catholic Church, leading to a hearing with the Bishop of London in 1377 to answer charges of heresy. He did not leave the Catholic Church, but he worked to reform the Church from the inside. Because of his teachings, Wycliffe was accused of being involved with the Peasants' Revolt of 1381, which resulted in his followers being forced out of Oxford.

The final years of Wycliffe's life included several trials, the completion of at least six books, and the translation of the Vulgate into English in 1382, which was the first English Bible. John Wycliffe died on December 31, 1384, and he was buried in the graveyard at Lutterworth Church. The Catholic Church excommunicated him thirty-one years after his death, and in 1428 his bones were exhumed, burned, and the ashes were thrown on the River Swift.

While the Catholic Church would not approve an English translation of the Bible, a French translation was a different story. In 1377 the Bible of Charles V of France was created and dedicated to the French king. Of course, the pope did reside in Avignon from 1309 to 1378 and he had a very strong presence in France during this period of time.

Initial research led me to believe that tension between Wycliffe and the Catholic Church was the result of his desire to print and distribute a Bible in the vernacular. Later research, however, revealed that there were other tensions, including Wycliffe's teaching that the government should seize the property of immoral clerics. For the most part, the English government supported and protected Wycliffe, except in his position on transubstantiation, which they did not support.

John Wycliffe was a man of great knowledge and commitment to Christ, the Church, and spreading the Word of God by making it easily accessible to the common man. He remained a part of his Church to the very end, but he argued for reforms that he believed would return it to a truer picture of the New Testament Church.

This book presents a Protestant perspective of the life of John Wycliffe. In studying Catholic websites, I find that he is remembered as a heretic who preached against the Church and caused a great deal of problems, perhaps chief among them his stance against the doctrine of transubstantiation, which may be the single most irreconcilable difference between Catholics and Protestants today.

The following are some quotes from John Wycliffe:

The Bible is for the government of the people, by the people, and for the people.

Englishmen learn Christ's law best in English. Moses heard God's law in his own tongue, so did Christ's apostles.

The gospel alone is sufficient to rule the lives of Christians everywhere...any additional rules made to govern men's conduct added nothing to the perfection already found in the Gospel of Jesus Christ.

The Catholic Church made every effort to destroy all written works of John Wycliffe, but his English version of the Bible (based on the Latin Vulgate) was distributed illegally by men involved in the "poor priest" movement, known as the Lollards. They wore long dark red robes, and they went about two by two preaching the importance of piety and the teachings of John Wycliffe. The Church declared them to be heretics, leading some of them to be burned alive. In 1408, the Archbishop of Canterbury, Arundel, decreed "that no man hereafter by his own authority translate any text of the scripture into English or any other tongue..." But the works of Wycliffe did survive and found their way into the hands of John Hus, an ordained priest who taught at the Charles University in Prague and agreed with Wycliffe on several matters of faith.

John Hus denounced abuses of the Church during his sermons, centering mainly on church discipline and practice as opposed to matters of theology, especially in the matter of selling indulgences, as one papal candidate was doing to raise money to challenge his rivals. In 1414 he was summoned to the Council in Constance, where his safety was guaranteed by the emperor. Under questioning, he declared that he had never held or taught several doctrines he was accused of, save that he did teach that the office of the pope did not exist by divine command, but was established by the Church (a view he shared with Thomas More).

Ultimately, John Hus was found guilty of heresy and he was burned alive at the stake on July 6, 1415. Like Wycliffe before him, John Hus left a lasting influence on those who followed his teachings. Followers of Hus and Jerome of Prague, also a martyr, eventually became known as the Czech Brethren, and later the Moravians. The Moravian Church exists to this day and was a strong influence on Martin Luther.

By the early fifteenth century, some priests were clearly asking for reform within the Catholic Church but were not being heard. The theological differences that Wycliffe and Hus had raised with the Church sound very much like those espoused by Martin Luther later in the sixteenth century. Wycliffe and Hus should be considered the founding fathers of the Reformation; for most Protestants, Church history doesn't even begin until 1517 or 1611.

Some of the research material I encountered included a warning that studying historical events from a strictly Protestant perspective may lead the reader to foster a dislike of Catholicism, which is not an intended, or even desired, purpose for this book. Students of the Old Testament are familiar with the failings of God's chosen people (the nation of Israel), so there should be no surprise that humans in the Catholic and Protestant churches have had similar experiences of falling away from God. During a study of the book of Kings with a fifth-grade Sunday school class, I started noticing how often the phrase "they would not listen" appeared; a quick Internet search revealed six times in 1 and 2 Kings, including in our memory verse of 2 Kings 17:14: "Nevertheless they would not hear, but stiffened their necks, like the necks of their fathers, who did not believe in the Lord their God."

Not listening to God seems to be a theme that permeates the study of Christian history, dating all the way back to Adam and Eve. Why don't we listen? God loves us—this we know for sure, so nothing good can come from ignoring Him.

Johann Gutenberg and the Printing Press

Perhaps the most overlooked person in history is Johann Gutenberg and the revolution he began with the invention of movable type and the printing press in 1456, which eventually helped bring books to the masses. Making books available to everyone should be considered the equivalent of inventing the Internet, as books had been written by hand up until that time and were very difficult to produce. The first book ever printed in human history was the Bible (the Latin Vulgate version), and a Gutenberg Bible is one of the rarest and most valuable books on the planet. The Gutenberg Bible is a masterpiece, even by today's standards. There are only twenty-two known copies left in the world. If a copy were to come available for auction, it would likely sell for more than $100 million.

Gutenberg's invention would prove to be a powerful tool used to bring the Bible to the masses only a few years later.

Important Events in Spain

In 1469, Ferdinand of Aragon married Isabella of Castile. Under their rule, Spain was believed to be one of the best-administered countries in Europe. They were able to take control of Granada in 1492, which had fallen to Muslim rule, and by 1525 all residents of Spain were officially Christian. History is not completely kind to King Ferdinand and Queen Isabella, as the Inquisition became a tool used during their rule to enforce religious unity. Jews and Muslims were required to convert to Christianity or leave the country. World history remembers Tomas de Torquemada as the Inquisitor General appointed in 1483, who, during his eighteen-year reign of terror, saw two thousand people burned alive and seventeen thousand people mutilated.

In 1492 King Ferdinand and Queen Isabella sponsored Christopher Columbus on his trip to discover a shorter route to the West Indies. Columbus had been rejected by the Portuguese king, after which he moved on to his native Genoa and then to Venice and finally to Spain to request funding. Once Granada was retaken, the monarchs in Spain agreed to fund his mission.

During the Dark Ages, God used Saint Patrick and Saint Columba to evangelize Ireland and Scotland. John Wycliffe completed the first English translation of the Bible. In the fifteenth century, Gutenberg invented the printing press, and the first book printed was the Bible. Columbus discovered new lands, which would lead to further expansion of Christianity into the western hemisphere. The Light of the World became brighter during the Dark Ages, and everything was in place for the continued expansion of Christianity.

Research points to the abuses of the Catholic Church in the fifteenth and sixteenth centuries, which is why men like Desiderius Erasmus, Martin Luther, and William Tyndale continued efforts to reform the Church from within. We need to understand that the horrific actions that the government and the Church took part in were normal for their day. The belief that a country should have a unified faith was prevalent at the time, although it usually led to the expulsion or execution of those who did not share or practice the "unified" faith.

Desiderius Erasmus

Born in Rotterdam, Holland, on October 27, 1466, Desiderius Erasmus was a priest (since about the age of twenty-five) and an extremely educated and learned man. He was known for writing several great literary works, the most significant of which was the product of a fifteen-year effort to edit an updated Greek New Testament in 1516. Erasmus's Greek Testament became known as the *Textus Receptus* and the foundation for translations of the Bible into German and English in the coming years, including the King James Bible of 1611. One would think that Erasmus would have been a vocal leader of the Reformation, but this was not the case. Erasmus, though in disagreement with the Catholic Church on several matters, including monasticism and making the Bible available in the vernacular, did not openly rebel against the pope and he never left the Church. Because of his writings, however, Erasmus was not popular with Church leaders. He was equally unpopular with followers of Martin Luther, who believed that he was being a coward and that he did not follow up his opinions with actions. A close look at Erasmus reveals that he was not without his faults, but he was certainly a man of convictions as evidenced by his writings.

> Erasmus stands as the supreme type of cultivated common sense applied to human affairs. He rescued theology from the pedantries of the Schoolmen, exposed the abuses of the Church, and did more than any other single person to advance the Revival of Learning.
> —www.historyguide.org/intellect/erasmus.html

Erasmus wrote several books of note, including *Handbook of a Christian Knight* in 1501, and *In Praise of Folly* in 1509. *In Praise of Folly* is considered to be one of the most important works of the Renaissance, and it also played a very important part in the Reformation.

In Praise of Folly

Erasmus penned his first copy of *In Praise of Folly* in one week while staying with his good friend Thomas More. (More was martyred in 1535 when King Henry VIII split from the Catholic Church and divorced Catherine of Aragon to marry Anne Boleyn.) The book is a satire whose

main character is Folly, a woman claiming to be mankind's greatest bene-
factor, representing freedom from care, youth, vitality, and happiness. *Folly*
praises self-deception and madness and moves to a satirical examination of
the abuses of Catholic doctrine and corrupt practices in various areas of the
Roman Catholic Church. Erasmus was careful to remain somewhat am-
biguous in the various editions of the book, as he did not want to set fire to
a revolution; he was only seeking reform. To Erasmus's surprise the book
became very popular and was translated into French, German, and English
(it was originally published in Latin). Pope Leo X found it to be funny.

Erasmus led a revolt that was not based on questioning of the truth of
traditional doctrine or hostility against the Church itself. Erasmus is considered by many to be the intellectual father of the Reformation; of him it
has been said: "Erasmus laid the egg; Luther hatched it." His criticisms of
the Catholic Church were made because of his belief that the Church was
succumbing to Scholasticism, and being pushed away from its evangelical
simplicity. He also believed the Church was becoming Pharisaical, overly
focused on ceremonies that stifled true religious devotion, which should actually be based on individual study and personal interpretation. Many of his
views became fundamental beliefs of the Protestant tradition.

Textus Receptus

Another editorial effort by Erasmus that had a great impact on the
Reformation was the annotated New Testament based on the original
Greek text, published in 1516, which came to be known as the received
text, or *Textus Receptus*. Erasmus was a Greek scholar, and he did a great
deal of research using the most ancient sources of the New Testament
available. As he was with other areas of Church practice, Erasmus was critical of the Latin Vulgate Bible, which he believed had become error-ridden
from its constant recopying over hundreds of years. Erasmus's New
Testament was the basis of some of the most famous Bibles ever later produced, including Luther's German Bible, Tyndale's English New
Testament, and the 1611 King James Bible.

The research pertaining to Erasmus was enlightening, to say the least,
as, to me, he is a kindred spirit. What is the most appropriate action when
you are in disagreement with the church that you love? The answer to unity
isn't simply to shut out those who are in disagreement with you; Christ
prayed that we would be one when He was in the Garden of Gethsemane,

and this is not accomplished by shutting out debate. Regarding Erasmus, John Mark Reynolds writes:

> Erasmus is a model for the man of faith who would follow reason… His mind was too broad for fundamentalism, which rejects reason, and too honest for intellectualism, which rejects revelation… [Erasmus] could never be described as anti-intellectual, but he did not worship worldly intellect.　　　　　*—The Great Books Reader*

An unexpected treasure was the letters between Erasmus and Martin Luther relating to doctrine, including that of free will. Luther had hoped Erasmus would join him in the movement, but Erasmus could not commit to the type of Reformation that Luther was seeking, one that would divide the Church that he loved. Erasmus was seeking to reform the Church in his own way.

October 31, 1517: Wittenberg

Martin Luther, like Wycliffe and Hus before him, was a priest who was disturbed by certain practices of the Catholic Church, specifically the practice of selling indulgences for the forgiveness of sins. He codified his objections into 95 theses (short statements), which he sent to his local bishop. He also posted a copy on the front door of Castle Church in Wittenberg on October 31, 1517. Luther was intending to create debate over the matter, and he thought the pope would come to his defense once he was aware of the abusive practice. Unfortunately, Luther was to find out that Pope Leo X had actually authorized the practice in Germany (which was not yet a country at that time). Copies of the 95 Theses were sent to the pope, and printers began distributing copies throughout the region. Luther's hope for a healthy debate on the subject of indulgences was instead met with the argument that the pope was infallible and had divine authority—and that indulgences were authorized by the pope himself. Luther was also reminded that John Hus had been burned at the stake for denying the pope's authority. Luther's response was to argue that support for the powers of the papacy could not be found in the Bible and that scripture was the supreme authority on such matters.

Luther's challenges to the practices of the Catholic Church expanded to include protests to prayers for the dead as well as the institution of the papacy. Core to Luther's beliefs were the ideas of justification by faith alone through Christ, that the deuterocanonical works (the Apocrypha) were not really part of the Bible and should not be considered scripture, and that the authority of the Bible was greater than that of the Church. He rejected the celibacy of the clergy and only practiced two of the seven sacraments: baptism and the Eucharist (the Lord's Supper).

When he was ordered to recant his opinions by the Roman emperor in 1521, Luther declared that he would not do so until he was "convinced by the testimony of the scripture." In 1521 Luther was excommunicated by the pope, and there was no going back; Luther would have to start a new church. Thus Lutheranism was born and the Protestant Reformation began to spread.

Other factors contributed to the widespread and immediate acceptance of the Reformation across Europe. Local rulers had desired independence from the Holy Roman Emperor, Charles V, for some time. There was unrest in Western Europe during this period, and many common people looked to Luther for leadership, but it was not Luther's desire to lead a great rebellion or a political movement.

Among the foundational principles that Luther espoused was "*Sola Scriptura*," Latin for "scripture alone." Luther stressed the authority of the Scriptures above all else, including Church tradition. In other words, he believed that the pope should not have final authority if a believer disagreed with his interpretation of scripture. The Catholic Church would argue that adherence to this doctrine resulted in the creation of thousands of Protestant denominations, each claiming to interpret the Scriptures based on the work of the Holy Spirit.

Luther and Erasmus:
Free Will—The Great Debate

In the spring of 2013, I took my family to see *Passages*, an extensive collection of biblical artifacts and their histories. *Passages* was sponsored by Steve Green, the president of Hobby Lobby, and it was an amazing display of historical artifacts of significant importance. The exhibit included multimedia displays, including a hypothetical conversation between Luther and Erasmus prior to October 31, 1517. I thank Steve Green for putting together such a quality exhibit relating to the history of the most famous book ever written.

Regarding the interaction between Erasmus and Luther, both wanted to see reform within the Church, but Erasmus was also trying to prevent a great division, while Luther, after publishing his 95 Theses, was dragged into a debate with the pope and was forced to challenge him openly.

Martin Luther and Desiderius Erasmus exchanged letters and debated what may be the most divisive topic in the current age (five hundred years later): the roles of grace and free will in salvation. It is well-known that Luther held Erasmus in high regard and that Erasmus hoped to persuade Luther to rejoin the Catholic Church and, in so doing, prevent what was to become a second great schism in the Church (the first having occurred in 1054 when the Orthodox Church split from the Church of Rome).

The 95 Theses posted on the church in Wittenberg make no mention of the subject of free will versus grace. This issue became an essential point in the Protestant Reformation, however, and was discussed in great length in correspondence exchanged between Luther and Erasmus over several years between 1520 and 1533. While this book is not intended to enter into the debate, nor will I take a position on the great theological topic of predestination, the subject cannot be ignored. Here we have two of the greatest minds of their time debating one of the great controversial topics of our day, predestination. Luther and Erasmus were not the first great theologians to debate this topic; Augustine had written extensively on the matter during the fourth and fifth centuries.

> Now we do not, when we make mention of these things, take away freedom of will, but we preach the grace of God... Do we then by grace make void free will? God forbid! Nay, rather we establish free will. For even as the law by faith, so free will by grace, is not made void, but established. For neither is the law fulfilled except by free will but by the law is the knowledge of sin, by faith the acquisition of grace against sin, by grace the healing of the soul from the disease of sin, by the health of the soul freedom of will, by free will the love of righteousness, by love of righteousness the accomplishment of the law.
>
> —*Augustine*

Thomas Aquinas also wrote on the matter of free will versus grace in the thirteenth century; he stated that "man has free choice, otherwise counsels, exhortations, commands, prohibitions, rewards, and punishments would be in vain."

In contrast, Wycliffe and Hus both believed in the doctrine of predestination, but they also believed that no person could actually know if they were among the elect.

In *Bondage of the Will*, Luther took the position that the corrupted human will has no ability to respond to God. He wrote:

> For if it is not ourselves, but God only, who works salvation in us, it follows that nothing we do before HIS working in us, avails unto salvation… However, with regard to God, and in all things pertaining to salvation or damnation, man has no free will, but is a captive, servant, and bondslave, either to the will of God, or to the will of Satan.

I am not a student of the teachings of Martin Luther, and I do not want to misrepresent him. Suffice it to say, however, that Luther was led to take action against inappropriate practices of the Catholic Church during the sixteenth century, and I believe him to be a great man who stood firm in his beliefs.

Erasmus took the position that many good men had disagreed on this subject in the past and that it was not an essential doctrine of the faith. The Catholic Church took a position similar to Erasmus. In 1597, the pope called in delegates that represented both schools of thought to debate the topic of grace versus free will. The debates lasted ten years, beginning with Pope Clement VIII, and carried on by Pope Paul V. In the end, neither school of thought was approved, and the debates ended. The pope ordered both sides to cease any attacks on the other's position and a compromise was accepted.

As a Protestant, I am interested to see that the Catholic Church has not suffered through the divisions that the issue of predestination has caused Protestants over the centuries; it continues to cause division to this very day. I pray that my Protestant brothers and sisters will take note of the unity practiced by the Catholic Church after ten years of debate and not allow the issue of predestination to continue bringing division to the Body of Christ. Amen.

In 1522, Martin Luther published a New Testament in German, translating it from Erasmus's second edition Greek New Testament. Luther's goal, like that of Wycliffe and Erasmus, was to make the Bible available to everyone, and he did what was necessary to get the Bible into the hands of the people of his native Germany. Luther's translation is believed to be one of the finest in the German language, and like the King James Version, it helped bring definition to its native language. It is still in use today.

Luther's New Testament was a tremendous success in Germany, and Lutheranism spread quickly. It is widely accepted that Luther never intended to create a great division within the Catholic Church. It took great courage to draft the 95 Theses and publish them, but most scholars believe that Luther expected to receive support from the Church in addressing the problems that he raised.

The response from the Church, however, was that Luther was mistaken in his views, because it was not possible he could be right and a thousand years of Church tradition could be wrong. I compare Luther to the prophets of the Old Testament. "They would not listen" is a recurring theme with God's people. Christian leaders are very reluctant to listen to other Christian leaders, but what if the pope had listened to Martin Luther in 1517 and addressed the 95 Theses? Things would be vastly different today. However, there is no going back at this point.

Luther's Love of Music

It would be a mistake to set forth a discussion of Martin Luther and exclude his great love of music. Luther believed music to be a gift from God and a means to spread "the Holy Gospel which now by the grace of God has risen anew." As he had done in translating his New Testament, Luther translated hymns into the vernacular, and congregational singing became another byproduct of the Reformation. Hymns also became a tool for education in doctrine, as well, in Lutheran schools. In 1586 a Jesuit teacher commented that after a year, he had been unable to teach village boys the words of the Lord's Prayer, but after teaching them to sing they learned the Apostle's Creed and the Ten Commandments in only a few hours.

Not all Protestants shared Luther's love of music during the worship service. Ulrich Zwingli, believed by many to be a co-founder of the Reformation movement, which he led in Switzerland, was himself an excellent musician, but he believed that the sensual nature of music was distracting from the pure Word of God. Calvinist churches, as well, believed music to be a distraction and limited its use during the worship service.

Erasmus and Luther were not the only men to take a stand against the

Church and the pope in the early sixteenth century. Like Wycliffe, Hus, Erasmus, and Luther, William Tyndale was a man of great intelligence who was compelled to stand against his Church and his pope on the matter of making the Bible available in the vernacular.

Desiderius Erasmus published a newly edited New Testament from the original Greek in 1516 using the oldest sources available at that time. Martin Luther translated Erasmus's Greek New Testament into German in 1522 and the complete Bible in 1534. Other translations soon followed, including those into French, Dutch, Italian, Spanish, and several other languages.

We strengthen our faith by sharing in the knowledge and wisdom of these men. How? We read their books and keep their memory alive.

8

William Tyndale

William Tyndale was educated at Oxford University, receiving a master's degree in 1515 at the age of twenty-one. An associate of Tyndale once commented that Tyndale was "so skilled in eight languages—Hebrew, Greek, Latin, Spanish, French, Italian, English, and German—that whichever he speaks, you might think it was his native tongue!"

Tyndale requested approval from the bishop in London to translate a new edition of the Bible. In 1524 King Henry VIII was Catholic (this would change in a few years), and he supported the position of the Church in disallowing an English translation of the Bible. For Tyndale, this position was not acceptable, however; he was determined that the Bible be made available to the common man in the vernacular. Tyndale was a priest, but he was once so frustrated by a fellow clergyman's comment that "we are better to be without God's laws than the pope's," he famously responded:

> I defy the pope and all his laws. If God spare my life ere many years, I will cause the boy that drives the plow to know more of the scriptures than you!

Unable to produce an English translation in his native country, Tyndale traveled to Wittenberg, Germany, to complete this work. It is believed that he met with Luther there. Tyndale would stay in Germany to complete his translation of the New Testament into English based primarily on Erasmus's Greek New Testament, as well as Luther's German translation, and he completed a partial edition in 1525 in Cologne. Unfortunately, Tyndale was forced to flee to Worms when his efforts were betrayed to the authorities; producing an English translation of the Bible was illegal at that time. Worms is where he finally completed his New Testament translation in 1526.

The Tyndale New Testament

Like Luther, Tyndale took positions that were contrary to the Catholic Church; among them was the concept of the priesthood of all believers, meaning that every Christian was, in fact, a priest and had the right to interpret Scripture for himself. Tyndale therefore translated several words differently from Jerome's Vulgate, including "elder" as opposed to "priest," "repent" as opposed to "penance," and "congregation" as opposed to "church." Tyndale's was the first New Testament actually printed in English.

Tyndale was in hiding and living out of the country when his New Testaments were smuggled into England in barrels and sacks of flour and corn. They were illegal in England, and they were burned publicly when found. The Church would buy all of the copies it could so they might be destroyed. Tyndale wrote to King Henry VIII and offered to return to England and submit to whatever punishment Henry decided if the king would only make the English New Testament freely available to his people. The king refused, but the demand for the English Bible was strong and would continue to grow. Tyndale was ultimately betrayed by his friend Henry Phillips (whose motive was money) in 1535, and he was imprisoned in Vilvorde Castle, six miles from Brussels, Belgium. Eventually Tyndale was tried for heresy, condemned, and on August 6, 1536, was strangled at the stake and his body burned. His last words were a prayer for King Henry VIII: "Lord, open the King of England's eyes."

William Tyndale paid with his life for translating the Bible into English and distributing copies to the people of England, but his efforts were not in vain. Tyndale's Bible was to have a profound and lasting impact on the English language and future English translations, including the 1611 King James Bible.

Not coincidentally, Tyndale had openly opposed Henry VIII's divorce from his first wife, Catherine of Aragon, as well as the king's planned wedding to Anne Boleyn. Others who openly opposed this divorce were also put to death, such as Thomas More, who also opposed the Reformation.

I recently visited a Catholic website to research their view of William Tyndale. The site pointed out that Tyndale was condemned not for translating the Bible into English, but because his translation was full of errors and heresy, as was the translation of John Wycliffe. The translations of the words "elder," "penance," and "congregation" carry great consequences for the authority of the Catholic Church. So, to this day, interpretation of scripture still divides the Catholic Church from the Protestant Church.

Will this division ever be bridged? With God, all things are possible.

The Real Father of the English Language

If you Google the question, *"Who was the father of the English language?"* the response will likely be *Geoffrey Chaucer*, whose great works include *The Canterbury Tales*. The name of William Tyndale was never mentioned during any of my English literature classes in high school or college. So you may wonder, Who would ever question Chaucer's significant contributions to the English language, or propose that Tyndale, whom most people have never heard of, should be considered in place of Chaucer as the father of the English language?

This is why knowledge of our Christian heritage is so very important— not to downplay the significant contributions of Chaucer, but to add to our knowledge of Tyndale. His memory is worthy of our time and effort.

Most of us have no knowledge that the Tyndale New Testament was relied upon by the translators of the King James Bible of 1611; studies have suggested the KJV New Testament is 83 percent the same as Tyndale's. Below is a listing of English translations of phrases from scripture that can be credited to Tyndale:

"Behold, the lamb of God."

"I am the way, the truth, and the life."

"In my father's house are many mansions."

"For thine is the kingdom and the power and the glory."

"Seek, and ye shall find."

"With God, all things are possible."

"Behold, I stand at the door and knock."

"The spirit is willing, but the flesh is weak."

"For my yoke is easy and my burden light."

This list is not exhaustive. The point is that Tyndale's contributions to the English language are grossly underappreciated. If you take his English translation of the Greek New Testament into consideration, his work has been read by ten thousand times as many readers as the works of Chaucer.

Tyndale completed translations of several books of the Old Testament, including the Pentateuch and the book of Jonah, before his work was disrupted by his arrest in 1535. Myles Coverdale completed Tyndale's work on the Old Testament, and on October 4, 1535, he published the first complete English Bible, known as the Coverdale Bible. Coverdale was a priest who shared Tyndale's belief that the Bible must be made available to the people of England in their own language, despite the objections of the Church.

Tyndale's dying prayer for the king of England would be answered just a few months later when the king broke from Rome and allowed the printing and distribution of the Coverdale Bible in 1537.

John Calvin and Reformed Theology

John Calvin was born in France in 1509 and received his education at the Universities of Paris, Orleans, and Bourges. While studying law at the University of Orleans, he became active in the cause of the Reformation, and in 1536 he published his landmark work, *Institutes of the Christian Religion*. Calvin's works emphasized the sovereignty of scripture and divine predestination.

Calvin lived in Geneva before being forced to leave because of his Protestant beliefs, but he was asked to return in 1541, when he became an influential spiritual and political leader using Protestant principles as a basis of government. In 1555 Calvin became the supreme authority in Geneva, which became the center of Protestantism. (Geneva has been nicknamed by some historians as the "Protestant Rome" during this period.) Calvin sent out pastors to Europe, Scotland, and England. Presbyterianism in Scotland, Puritans in England, and the Reformed Church in the Netherlands owe their origins to Calvin's work in Geneva. Several historians believe that Calvin was somewhat intolerant of beliefs that differed from his own. During the first five years of his rule in Geneva, fifty-eight people were executed; the most famous execution was that of convicted heretic Michael Servetus.

Calvin founded the Genevan Institute of Reformed Studies in 1559, which quickly became an international center of theological study. Today the school is known as the University of Geneva, and, like most major universities founded on Christian doctrine and beliefs, has unfortunately become a secular institution in modern times. Calvin died in 1564 and is buried in an unmarked grave in Geneva.

Some claim that Geneva was operated as a police state under Calvin, while others believe that Calvin's goal was to have a government and city as close to a biblical basis as possible. Under Calvin's leadership, Geneva became the center of Reformed Theology from Great Britain throughout Europe. His influence on Christianity in the form of Calvinism continues to be strong in the Protestant Church; even so-called Reformed churches are linked to Calvin. This is interesting, because all Protestant churches are actually "Reformed" from the broader perspective of the Reformation movement.

The Jesuits

The Society of Jesus, later to be known as the Jesuits, was founded by a Spanish knight named Ignatius Loyola. He developed an interest in spirituality while recovering from a battle wound he received in 1521. He went on a pilgrimage to Jerusalem, then studied theology in Spain and in Paris. Loyola had dedicated his life to Christ and found like-minded friends willing to do the same, including taking vows of poverty, chastity, and obedience. In 1539 they formed the Society of Jesus, which was approved by Pope Paul III in 1540. Jesuits were all priests and completely obedient to the pope; they were also very well trained. The Church used the Jesuits to oppose Protestantism through various means, including theological debate. To engage in such debate, Jesuits needed to be well-educated, and Loyola worked to build a school for non-members of the Society to educate them in understanding Christianity from the perspective of the Jesuits. By the time Loyola died in 1536, thirty-five Jesuit schools in Europe offered an excellent education at no cost, because Loyola believed that education should be available to everyone.

The Jesuits were very successful in limiting the rapid growth of Protestantism in Lithuania, Poland, and Ukraine. They would also play a role in planting missions in North and South America, and they made significant contributions in the fields of science and exploration.

The Anabaptists

The Anabaptist denomination can trace its beginnings back to Zurich, Switzerland, in 1525, and these believers were somewhat radical for that day. The name *Anabaptist* refers to their belief that baptism should occur only after an individual's profession of faith in Christ. Infant baptism, as practiced by the Catholic and Lutheran churches, was not valid for the Anabaptists; therefore believers needed to be re-baptized when they came of age and belief in Christ. They also developed a "congregational" form of government for their church, believing that members of the entire congregation, not simply the priests, should participate in all of the decisions of the body. Protestants and Catholics both warred against the Anabaptists during this period, yet the movement grew and gathered strength. Anabaptist leader Menno Simons traveled throughout northern Europe; his influence was powerful, and churches reflecting his teachings were known as "Mennonite."

The greatest challenge in presenting the significant events of the Reformation is that so many different significant changes occurred concurrently. Remember, William Tyndale was executed on October 6, 1536, and he prayed that "God would open the king of England's eyes." That king was Henry VIII, and God would answer Tyndale's dying prayer.

The English Reformation and King Henry VIII

Henry the VIII is primarily remembered for having six wives: Two were executed, he divorced two, one died, and the last was widowed when Henry died. Why did he have six wives? The king desired to have a male heir. Henry and his first wife, Catherine of Aragon, had a daughter named Mary. Catherine was the daughter of Queen Isabella I and King Ferdinand II of Spain, the monarchs who sponsored Christopher Columbus's expedition to the New World. Catherine was also highly regarded by the people as well as great scholars such as Erasmus and Thomas More. However, she was not able to bear King Henry the son that he so desperately desired; thus the king sought an annulment to the marriage from Pope Clement VII. Unfortunately for Henry VIII, Catherine was also the aunt of the Holy Roman Emperor at the time, Charles V, and the pope would not grant Henry the annulment he sought. The problem was that Henry had already decided to marry one of his daughter Mary's ladies-in-waiting,

Anne Boleyn. Henry and Anne were married in a secret ceremony in January 1533. But until the end of her life in 1536, Catherine referred to herself as the true wife of King Henry VIII.

The Education of Christian Women, written by Juan Luis Vives, claimed that women had the right to an education; this project was commissioned by and dedicated to Catherine. Catherine was also a member of the Third Order of Saint Francis and she was committed to the Catholic Church.

King Henry needed his marriage to Anne Boleyn to be recognized by the Church. Therefore, any man who refused to recognize his marriage to Anne was executed, including William Tyndale and Thomas More. Henry's ultimate response was to break away from the Church of Rome and declare that from then on, the Church of England would be under the control of the king of England rather than the pope's. Sweeping changes followed, including the Act of Supremacy in 1534, which declared that all churchmen were to swear an oath recognizing the king as the head of the Church. Monasteries that remained loyal to the pope were shut down, their buildings destroyed, and their belongings confiscated. Henry's advisor, Thomas Cranmer, became the Archbishop of Canterbury and officially declared Henry's marriage to Catherine null and void on May 23, 1533. Five days later, Henry's marriage to Anne was declared good and valid, and on June 1, 1533, Anne was crowned the queen of England.

Further distancing himself from the Catholic Church, King Henry authorized the printing of an English translation of the Bible, and ordered that one copy of this translation be made available to all nine thousand churches in England. In 1537 Henry allowed for the distribution of the Matthew's Bible, which included translations from the Coverdale Bible. In 1539, Henry licensed Coverdale to produce the "Great Bible." Based largely on Tyndale's work, the Great Bible was the first translation of the Scriptures to be authorized by the king and placed in all churches in England. Tyndale's prayer had been answered: The people of England could now have access to a Bible in their own language for the first time without fear of arrest.

Henry and Anne celebrated the birth of their first and only child on September 7, 1533, a daughter, whom they named Elizabeth. Three miscarriages followed, and by March of 1536 Henry had begun courting Jane Seymour. As the famous history goes, Henry had Anne arrested and tried for high treason, including charges of adultery, incest, and witchcraft. Anne was imprisoned in the Tower of London, she was subsequently tried on May 14, and ultimately beheaded on May 19, 1536. Queen Anne Boleyn is remembered as being a friend to the Reformation movement in England, a martyr, and the mother of Queen Elizabeth I. It is believed that Anne gave Henry a copy of Tyndale's *The Obedience of the Christian Man* with certain passages marked as "worthy of the king's knowledge." One main point of the book was that men were accountable to God, not the pope. Anne Boleyn also owned a copy of Tyndale's New Testament.

Henry married Jane Seymour on May 20, 1536—one day after Anne's beheading. Jane Seymour finally bore Henry a son on October 12, 1537, but she died of childbirth complications a few days later on October 24. This son was the future King Edward VI. Jane was the only one of Henry's wives to receive a queen's funeral. After the death of Jane, Henry was single for two years, but he eventually married Anne of Cleves on January 6, 1540, then divorced her seven months later.

In July 1540, the forty-nine-year-old King Henry VIII married nineteen-year-old Kathryn Howard, the first cousin of Anne Boleyn. Henry had gained weight by this time, and he was dealing with an ulcerated leg. He referred to his new young wife as a "rose without a thorn." Unfortunately, evidence that Kathryn was involved in extramarital affairs began to mount. Henry did not want to believe the accusations, but the evidence became sufficient enough to charge her with adultery, and on February 13, 1542, she was executed and then laid to rest near her cousin, Henry's previous wife Anne Boleyn.

Henry's sixth and final wife was Katherine Parr, whom he married on July 12, 1543. Interestingly, Thomas Seymour, the brother of Henry's third wife, Jane, also pursued her as a wife. King Henry VIII died on January 28, 1547 and was succeeded by his only son, King Edward VI.

King Henry VIII's reign lasted from 1509 through 1547, and due to his numerous marriages, a split from the Catholic Church took place, and the Anglican Church, or the Church of England, was born. Henry's heirs include the future King Edward VI, Queen Mary, and Queen Elizabeth I. King Edward VI was crowned the king of both England and Ireland on January 28, 1547, at the age of nine. Edward was the first monarch in England to be raised as a Protestant.

Under Edward, the Anglican Church shifted toward a more Protestant form of doctrine. In 1549 the *Book of Common Prayer*, written by Thomas

Cranmer, the Archbishop of Canterbury, was composed; it included a collection of prayers and liturgies for use in English churches. Some historians consider the *Book of Common Prayer* a unifying factor for most English churches, as it took a middle route between Catholicism and Protestantism, but others believed the book actually widened the rift between Rome and England. Under the reign of Edward VI, which lasted from January of 1547 to the summer of 1553, Protestantism was established as the state religion. By 1553, however, Edward had become ill, and when he realized that his illness was terminal, he devised a plan of succession that would prevent England from returning to Catholicism; he named his cousin, Lady Jane Grey, as his successor, excluding his half sisters, Mary and Elizabeth, from the monarchy.

Lady Jane Grey, also known as the Nine Days' Queen, was crowned the queen of England on July 10, 1553, but she was deposed nine days later on July 19. Jane Grey was considered one of the most learned women of her day—and she was Protestant. Unfortunately for her, under pressure from Mary—the daughter of Catherine of Aragon and Henry VIII—the Privy Council changed sides and proclaimed Mary as queen on July 19. Jane was imprisoned for high treason and later executed. This would be the first of many executions associated with Queen Mary (who has been remembered in history as "Bloody Mary" due to her penchant for capital punishment for those who opposed her reign).

Mary would reign for only five years, but she would leave an indelible mark on history as she worked to reverse the Protestant Reformation in England and return the country to Catholicism. In 1554 Mary became betrothed to King Philip of Spain, thus making him the king of England as well as of Spain from 1556 to 1558. Under Queen Mary's rule, there were over 280 public executions of Protestants, the first of which was John Rogers on February 4, 1555. Rogers had been a friend of William Tyndale's, and he is credited with translating the second complete English Bible in 1537 under the pseudonym of Thomas Matthews. Thomas Cranmer, who had worked to accomplish the annulment of Mary's mother's marriage to King Henry VIII, was also executed in 1556. Not surprisingly, another outcome of Mary's reign was the exodus of several Protestant theologians to Geneva.

Geneva and the English Bible

It is believed that at least eight hundred Protestants fled to Geneva during Queen Mary's reign and awaited her death before returning; she finally died on November 17, 1558. Protestants living in Geneva believed there was a need for a new Bible translation, and they began work on what would eventually become the Geneva Bible, first published in 1560. About 80 percent of the New Testament found in the Geneva Bible was based on Tyndale's earlier translation. However, the Geneva Bible is the first English Bible in which all of the Old Testament was translated from the original Hebrew. The Geneva Bible was also the first Bible to have numbered verses and be printed in Roman type (still used today); it would include elaborate commentaries, wood-cut maps, an introduction by John Calvin, and the apocryphal books, which were placed at the end of the Old Testament, and it was known as the first study Bible in history.

The quality of the Geneva Bible was exceptional, and it quickly became the most popular English Bible of its day, preferred even over the Great Bible. The importance of the Geneva Bible cannot be overstated with respect to its influence on Christianity in England. It was also the very first Bible printed in Scotland.

Queen Mary died before the Geneva Bible was completed, and a new, Protestant queen was crowned, thus allowing the return of the Protestants who had left during Queen Mary's bloody reign.

Queen Elizabeth I and the Elizabethan Era

At the age of twenty-five, Elizabeth I became the queen of both England and Ireland on September 17, 1558, and one of her first acts as a monarch was to establish the English Protestant Church. It is very interesting to examine the evolving doctrine of the Church of England under Queen Elizabeth's rule, as it contained elements of both the Catholic and Protestant faiths; historians believe this occurred in order to accommodate the Catholics of England. Though Elizabeth was Protestant, she would not embrace the more radical reforms that were sought by the Puritans, who wanted the removal of all liturgies associated with Catholicism.

Elizabeth's forty-four-year reign is considered one of great stability and success in England during a time of great unrest in Europe. The Elizabethan Era produced the works of Shakespeare and Marlowe, the defeat of the Spanish Armada in 1588, and extensive seafaring exploration by Sir Francis Drake. Elizabeth's government was more moderate than either that of her father (King Henry VIII) or half sister (Mary I); one of her mottos was "*video et taceo*" ("I see, and say nothing").

The faith of Elizabeth I should never be in question. Below is an excerpt from one of her prayers:

> This is my state. Now where is my comfort? In the depth of my misery I know no help (O Lord), but the height of thy mercy, who hast sent thine only Son into the world to save sinners. This God of my life and life of my soul, the King of all comfort, is my only refuge. For his sake therefore, to whom thou hast given all power, and wilt deny no petition, hear my prayers. Turn thy face from my sins (O Lord) and thine eyes to thy handiwork. Create a clean heart, and renew a right spirit within me. Order my steps in thy word, that no wickedness have dominion over me, make me obedient to thy will, and delight in thy law. Grant me grace to live godly and to govern justly: that so living to please thee, and reigning to serve thee I may ever glorify thee, the Father of all goodness and mercy. To whom with thy dear Son, my only Saviour, and the Holy Ghost my Sanctifier, three persons and one God: be all praise, dominion and power, world without end.

Still, friction grew between Elizabeth and the Catholic Church, as in the eyes of the pope she was an illegitimate child and not the true queen of England. In an official communication dated 1570, the pope wrote:

> ... Elizabeth, the pretended queen of England and the servant of crime...with whom as in a sanctuary the most pernicious of all have found refuge... She has followed and embraced the errors of the heretics... We declare her to be deprived of her pretended title to the crown... We charge and command all and singular the nobles, subjects, peoples...that they do not dare obey her orders, mandates and laws...
> —*Regnans in Excelsis*, the papal bull deposing Elizabeth, 1570

Catholics were not allowed to hold positions of power in England during Elizabeth's reign, as they were considered potential traitors. Many Catholics in England believed that Mary (queen of Scots) was the true queen of England. In 1568 Mary had been deposed as the queen of Scotland, replaced by her one-year-old son, James VI, and she fled to England. In England her name became associated with plots to kill Elizabeth, and she was eventually executed on February 8, 1587.

The Age of Confessionalism

The Reformation gave birth to the Lutheran, Reformed (including Presbyterian), Anglican, and Anabaptist denominations during the sixteenth century. But as each church group became formalized and established, they drew up creeds, or "confessions," that outlined their various positions and doctrines. This era of the Church is sometimes called the "age of confessionalism." As church groups further defined themselves, new movements began that further divided the body of Christ.

The Catholic Response to the Reformation

From the Protestant perspective, the Reformation was a time of great Catholic persecution against believers who were raising concerns about certain practices of the Church, or who desired a Bible translation in the vernacular. Religious wars raged between Catholics and Protestants, resulting in the deaths of countless numbers of believers; this book touches on only a few of these wars. Erasmus and Luther sought reform from within the Church, but did their efforts bear any fruit? The answer is yes: The Catholic Church did make an effort to address their concerns, beginning in the era of Pope Paul III in 1534, including the approval of the Jesuits in 1540, and continuing in 1545 at the Council of Trent.

The Council of Trent

The Council of Trent met twenty-five times between December 1545 and December 1563. These meetings resulted in reforms that included condemnation of the sale of indulgences, immorality of clergy, and nepotism; it also defined Church teachings in the areas of tradition, sacraments, the Eucharist in the Holy Mass, the veneration of the saints, and many others. Such reforms helped to reduce the open rebellion that was occurring in Europe and reverse the trend of losing great numbers of the population to Protestantism. In the end, the Council did not give any ground to Protestants in the area of doctrine; although they agreed that personal faith was necessary for salvation, they did not believe it was sufficient. The Council also rejected the Protestant belief that the Bible should be the sole source for doctrine and was more authoritative than Church tradition. Instead they maintained that the Church and the Bible formed a whole, undivided body of teaching. The Council of Trent marked a milestone in the Catholic Church with respect to its self-understanding.

The Saint Bartholomew's Day Massacre:
August 24, 1572

In 1572, tensions grew between the Catholics and the Protestant Huguenots. The Huguenots were French Protestants who aspired to the writings of John Calvin and were very critical of the pope and the Catholic Church, believing vast reforms were needed. The Saint Bartholomew's Day Massacre occurred during a period of civil infighting known as the French Wars of Religion (1562–98).

As the incident has been recorded, approximately five thousand Protestants had traveled to Paris at the express invitation of the royal family to attend a wedding between Margaret, the Catholic sister of the king of France, to the Protestant Henry III of Navarre (the future Henry IV of France). Tradition holds that the queen, when told—and apparently convinced—that the Protestants planned to murder her daughter, became outraged and ordered that all Protestants be killed.

At 3:00 A.M. on August 24, 1572, the city gates were locked and soldiers were turned loose throughout the city. Estimates of the carnage vary greatly, but between thirty and seventy-five thousand Protestants are believed to have been massacred that night, including many children.

When news of the massacre reached the pope, he believed it to be an act of divine intervention, and jubilation took place at the Vatican. A special commemorative medal was struck to honor the occasion, and Italian artist Vasari was commissioned to paint a mural of the massacre, which hangs in the Vatican to this day. The king of Spain is said to have laughed for the only time on record upon hearing of the massacre. However, the rest of Europe was appalled, and an international crisis ensued. The ambassador from England to France had barely escaped with his life. Though the incident was not a unique event, it is believed to be the worst religious massacre of that century.

In 1593, English playwright Christopher Marlowe wrote a strongly anti-France, anti-Catholic play titled *The Massacre at Paris*. A 1966 episode of the British television series *Doctor Who* is also entitled "The Massacre of St. Bartholomew's Eve." This episode is missing from the BBC archives, but it is available in audio form.

Foxe's Book of Martyrs

Foxe's Book of Martyrs is referred to by some Bible scholars as the second most influential theological book ever printed, second only to the Bible, and it is an important part of our Christian heritage. To this day, John Foxe's record represents the most complete compilation of Christian martyrs, covering the period from the first century through the mid-sixteenth century. Unfortunately, the first two editions of the book had a distinctly anti-Catholic tone; Catholic writers criticized its accuracy and Foxe was forced to make corrections. First published in English in 1563, just a few years following the reign of Queen Mary, the book was immensely popular, but it intensified dislike of Catholics because of its content, especially the details of the execution of Protestants that occurred during Mary's reign, as well as the Spanish Inquisition. Foxe based his research on authentic documents, including reports from trials and statements from friends of those who were persecuted.

Among the martyrs of the early Church included in Foxe's book is Perpetua. Perpetua was a twenty-two-year-old nursing mother who was sentenced to death for refusing to recant her Christian beliefs over the objections of her father and the governor, who desired to free her. They both implored her to recant for the sake of her child. This particular execution took place in second-century Rome, when, because of their faith, Christians were put to death in the coliseum arena.

Foxe's book also includes details of the martyrdom of the Disciples of Christ during the first century. While *Foxe's Book of Martyrs* is considered a very important part of Protestant history, especially in England during the Reformation, many Catholics challenge the accuracy of the book to this day and they believe it to be a source of English anti-Catholicism.

During Queen Elizabeth's reign, significant friction between Catholics and Protestants continued, although she brought to an end the nine-plus-years-long war with Catholic subjects in Ireland who had defied her authority. Protestants tend to remember Elizabeth with great admiration, although some historians point out that the Church of England, which she established, included a great many Catholic liturgies and did not address concerns of the Puritans. Queen Elizabeth's reign came to an end on March 24, 1603; her chosen successor was King James VI of Scotland, who became King James I of England that same day.

The Douay-Rheims Bible

Many Catholics fled England during the reign of Queen Elizabeth, just as Protestants had done under Queen Mary. The Douay-Rheims Bible was the product of members of the English College in Douai, France, in service to the Catholic Church and as a response to the Protestant Reformation; it is largely an English translation of the Latin Vulgate. The New Testament version of this translation was first published in the French city of Reims in 1582 and smuggled into England. The entire Douay-Rheims Bible was not published until 1610.

Clergyman John Knox, who had spent time with John Calvin while in Geneva, led Church reforms in Scotland. Knox was a fiery preacher who frequently clashed with Queen Mary I of England. He is considered to be the founder of the Presbyterian Church in Scotland, just as John Calvin is considered the founder of Reformed theology, to which Presbyterianism adheres.

In closing this chapter on the Reformation, which most Protestants celebrate as the beginning of a new era of religious freedom and empowerment of the Christian Church, I offer the Catholic view of this period of history: While visiting a Catholic website, I notice the phrases "great religious revolt" and "abandonment of principal Christian beliefs" in referencing the Reformation.

The five-hundred-year anniversary of the beginning of the Protestant Reformation will take place on October 31, 2017; perhaps at that time a revival of interest in the history of this significant event will take place.

The newly crowned king of England, King James I, would be faced with the important decision of which Bible would become the official Bible of the Church in his country. The Puritans were using the Geneva Bible, and they wanted the Church to function independently of the state, just as the Presbyterian Church did in Scotland; both of these groups held to doctrine that was contrary to the position of the Anglican Church. But because James I had been raised as a member of the Protestant Church of Scotland, Puritans were hoping that this new king of England would be favorable to their proposed changes to the Anglican Church; however, they were in for a surprise.

9

The King James Bible

If the seed of desire to learn where I came from was planted during my college study of *Sir Gawain and the Green Knight*, then that seed sprouted when I developed a course covering the history of the English Bible for my church. The more I read on the topic, the more I wanted to learn. Frankly, I wasn't aware that any other version of the Bible existed before the translation of the King James Version (KJV) Bible of 1611. Like the stories told of the history of the Septuagint, the Dead Sea Scrolls, the Latin Vulgate, and the first English translation of the Bible, the history behind the KJV translation is intriguing and, in my opinion, an essential component of our Christian heritage.

Prior to the creation of the KJV, numerous English translations were available, including the Geneva Bible. But a great debate arose as to which translation should become the standard for the Church of England. Much was at stake in England for the Puritans, who were looking for change during the reign of King James I. John Rainolds, the president of Corpus Christi College and believed to be one of the most brilliant men of his day, was a champion for Puritan beliefs and he desired an audience with the king.

Queen Elizabeth did not announce her successor until very close to her death, which was a strategically wise move; if a successor was announced too early, it could have led to the premature death of the queen. Most of her council believed that James VI of Scotland would be the queen's choice, as she had stated:

> I told you my seat has been the seat of kings, and I will have no rascal to succeed; who should succeed me but a king?

Legend has it that when Elizabeth lost the power of speech, she touched her crown, which was interpreted by those in attendance that she

wished her successor to be one who already wore a crown. James was therefore crowned the king of England within eight hours of Elizabeth's death
on March 24, 1603. One of the first matters King James I would need to
deal with was his response to the Millenary Petition, said to have contained
at least one thousand signatures of Puritans who were expressing concerns
about abuses in the Church of England. James responded by calling for a
conference at the Hampton Court Palace in January 1604.

What the Puritans had failed to realize, however, was that although
James had been raised as a Protestant, he believed strongly in the divine
rights of kings. He disliked the idea of independence sought by the
Presbyterians and the Puritans, along with their Geneva Bible. James did
not plan to make any changes to Elizabeth's previous approach to religious
rifts in England: *via media* (the "middle way"). Under Queen Elizabeth, the
Church had a Catholic appearance and a fundamentally Protestant doctrine. She once said to her Privy Council: "There is only one Jesus Christ.
The rest is an argument over trifles." Understanding how King James intended to govern makes the outcome of the conference at Hampton Court
Palace very logical, as well as historically significant.

An excellent account of the details of the conference can be found in
Majestie, by David Teems. The king was somewhat intolerant of the
Puritans, but he listened to their spokesman, John Rainolds. King James
occasionally asked Bancroft to tone down his rhetoric when he became
critical of Rainolds, who, before the conference would close, would make a
simple but history-making suggestion:

> …moved his Majesty, that there might be a new translation of the
> Bible, because those which were allowed in the reigns of Henry the
> eighth, and Edward the sixth, were corrupt and not answerable to the
> truth of the Original.

Bancroft responded emotionally, "If every man's humor was followed,
there would be no end of translating!" But the king approved of Rainold's
suggestion, and disagreeing with Bancroft, admitted that he:

> …could never yet see a Bible well translated in English; but I think
> that, of all, that of Geneva is the worst. I wish some special pains were
> taken for an uniform translation, which should be done by the best

learned men in both Universities, then reviewed by the Bishops, presented to the Privy Council, lastly ratified by the Royal authority, to be read in the whole Church, and none other.

King James disliked the Geneva Bible because of its Calvinistic notes, which he believed to be derogatory of earthly kings. Bancroft, who had been critical of the suggestion of a new translation, was put in charge of the project. Essentially he project was intended to revise the Bishop's Bible, which was first published in 1568 and last revised in 1602. Part of the instructions to the translators, which were prepared by Bancroft, was that the Bishop's Bible only be altered when the "truth demanded it." One of Bancroft's more interesting instructions was that the word *tyrant* did not appear in the new translation.

There are many excellent books that detail the translation process of the King James Bible, including Donald Brake's *A Visual History of the English Bible*. Brake is also a collector of Bibles and extremely knowledgeable of the history of the Bible translations.

The teams working on the King James Bible consisted of fifty-four highly qualified translators, including the leader, who were geographically dispersed. Puritan John Rainolds was selected to be on one of the teams. In 1605 and 1606, they engaged in private research. Work then began in 1607, was completed in 1611, and made use of earlier versions including Tyndale's (1526), Coverdale's (1535), Matthew's (1537), the Great Bible (1539), the Geneva Bible (1560), and the Bishop's Bible (1602). After four years of diligent work, the product of the translation team—our King James Bible—is considered by many to be the finest English translation ever accomplished, and it has greatly influenced English culture for hundreds of years.

In *Majestie,* author David Teems summarizes the results of the translation as follows (Teems's quote is followed by a quote from the preface of the King James Bible):

In truth, the new Bible was not a translation at all, but a revision. It was a patchwork quilt, with all the finest elements of its former voices stitched together. The whole intent was summed up in the preface to the 1611 version of the King James Bible (original spelling):

Truly (good Christian Reader) we neuer thought from the beginning, that we should need to make a new Translation, nor yet to make a bad one a good one…but to make a good one better, or out of many good ones, one principal good one, not iustly to be excepted against; that hath bene our indeauour, that our marke.

Here is more from the preface of the KJVB:
Happy is the man that delights in Scripture, and thrice happy that meditates in it day and night. But how can men meditate in that which he cannot understand? How shall he understand that which is kept close in an unknown tongue?

At more than eleven thousand words, the preface of the King James Bible is lengthy, but it is a masterpiece in itself and warrants a complete reading. The excellence of the translation, or revision, is beyond measure. I love the humility of the translators and their written goal to make a good translation better. Most importantly, they have provided the reader with a Bible they could actually understand. This may be a message to translators yet to come: There was no intent to open the hornets' nest of "King James Only" versus other translations. No doubt my generation has lived to see some very poor "translations" that go well beyond simply using the vernacular. We need to have a basic understanding of the translation we choose for study. The prefaces of most Bible translations include important information about the source of the translation.

The copyright of the King James Bible is unique: It is held by the British Crown and is still in force in the United Kingdom. Despite some theories that have been circulated, profit is actually made from the licensing of the King James Bible in the United Kingdom.

The efforts to complete the King James Bible were significant, the product was excellent and history making, but shockingly, it almost never happened due to a plot to kill the king and members of Parliament.

The Gunpowder Plot of 1605

Catholics living in England had hoped that King James I might provide some relief and tolerance as opposed to Queen Elizabeth's reign. Unfortunately, there was would be no relief for Catholics; therefore a small group of dissenters, led by Guy Fawkes, rented a house right next door to the House of Parliament and managed to get dozens of barrels of gunpowder smuggled into the cellar below. If their plot had been successful, the House of Parliament, the House of Lords, and King James I himself would have been blown to pieces at the same time. The plot was uncovered, however, the conspirators were executed, and a celebration on November 5 each year has been held ever since, which includes fireworks and the burning of an effigy of Guy Fawkes.

Needless to say, tensions ran high between Catholics and Protestants in England after details of the gunpowder plot became known. Protestants believed it was God's divine intervention that had saved King James I, Parliament, and the King James Bible. Although anti-Catholic legislation was introduced soon after the plot was foiled, King James I still allowed several devout Catholics to retain high offices during his reign.

Zondervan's *Handbook to the History of Christianity* provides an excellent recap of the post-Reformation period:

> At the start of the sixteenth century, there was a single Christian church in Europe. One hundred years later, there were four major ones. The Roman Catholic Church remained firm in most of the southern half of the continent, including Italy, Spain, most of France and southern German states. The Lutheran Churches...held the northern German states and Scandinavia. The Church of England remained the only legitimate church in England. The Reformed Churches...spread the Calvinist message across Europe, dominated Switzerland, the Netherlands and Scotland and had a strong minority presence in France.

Arminianism

Arminianism, the counterpart to Calvinism, is the term given to the teachings of Dutch theologian Jacobus Arminius. It was first articulated in the Remonstrance, a statement of theology that was signed by forty-five ministers in 1610.

Luther and Erasmus debated the idea of free will extensively, and the Catholic Church discussed the matter over a ten-year period without reaching a resolution. In other words, the Catholic Church did not let the issue become divisive as Protestants have.

Five articles were outlined in the Remonstrance of 1610 regarding the beliefs of the followers of Arminius: 1) conditional election (faith is necessary), 2) unlimited atonement, 3) total depravity, 4) resistible grace, and 5) the possibility of apostasy. Regarding the possibility of apostasy, or "falling away from the faith," Arminius himself stated he had never taught that a true believer could fall away from the faith, only that certain scripture passages seem to "wear this aspect." The Articles of Remonstrance went on to state that no believer could be plucked from Christ's hand, and that the matter of falling away required more study.

One famous response to the Articles of Remonstrance resulting from the synod held in the Netherlands in 1618, condemned the doctrines and outlined the Orthodox Reformed faith in five doctrines. Using the acronym TULIP, the doctrine is summarized as: 1) total depravity, 2) unconditional election, 3) limited atonement, 4) irresistible grace, and 5) the perseverance of the saints (otherwise known as the "once saved, always saved" doctrine).

The single similarity between the two doctrines is total depravity, which would be hard to argue against with any knowledge of history and current events. One difference between the doctrines involves the nature of election, which Arminians believe requires faith whereas Calvinists would argue no human effort is required. Another difference is the nature of grace: Arminians would argue that humans have free will to accept or reject God's grace, while Calvinists would argue that God's grace is given only to the elect and irresistibly leads to salvation.

This summary is intended to simplify the basic principles and differences between these two doctrinal positions. The differences between Arminianism and Calvinism will likely continue to be a source of great debate until the Second Coming of Christ; after that great day, however, the differences will no longer matter.

Puritans and Separatists

The Puritans, led by John Rainolds, had asked for reforms within the Church of England during an audience with the newly crowned King James I, but for the most part, they were met with no success. Despite this setback, they continued to seek changes, including the removal of Catholic elements in church services as well as lax standards of public behavior including drunkenness and the failure to properly keep the Sabbath.

Puritans believed the Church of England could be reformed from within, while Separatists believed they were elected by God for salvation and would face contamination if they worshipped with those outside their own church. In 1608, a group of Separatists moved to Holland, where there was more religious tolerance at that time than in England. Once in Holland, this group became known as Pilgrims. They feared for their children in Holland, and in 1620, they sailed for America on the *Mayflower*. Before leaving for the New World, the Pilgrims founded what would become one of the largest Protestant denominations in the New World, the Baptists.

The First Baptist Church

History credits former Anglican priest John Smyth as founder of the Baptist denomination while he was living in Amsterdam with other Separatists who had left England. In 1609 Smyth wrote *The Character of the Beast*, in which he stated that infants were not to be baptized and that "Antichristians converted are to be admitted into the true Church by baptism." Smyth was convinced from reading the Scriptures that infants would not be damned should they die, even without baptism. Thomas Helwys is considered a cofounder of the Baptist denomination, and along with Smyth, he established a Baptist Church in England in 1612. General Baptists believe that Christ's atonement extends to all people, while Particular Baptists reflect the Reformed theology of John Calvin and believe that atonement was only provided for the elect.

For many Christians, the history of the Bible begins with the publication of the King James Version of the Bible in 1611. Yet to ignore the important history that preceded its publication would be a mistake. We strengthen our faith and appreciate our connection to our brothers and sisters in Christ by cultivating a basic understanding of the Reformation and the publication of a Bible in a language other than Latin—important historical events that are part of our Christian heritage.

10

The New World

Separatists who had immigrated to Holland were not realizing the life they had hoped for, and they decided to migrate yet again to the newly colonized world across the Atlantic in New England. Considering themselves to be pilgrims to a new land, they sought and obtained permission from King James to found a new settlement working with the Virginia Company. The Pilgrims decided that William Brewster would lead their group, and they chartered the *Mayflower* and the *Speedwell* for their voyage. Unfortunately the *Speedwell* began to leak water and had to return to England. The *Mayflower* left England on September 6, 1620, arrived in Provincetown on November 11, and anchored in Plymouth Harbor on December 16, 1620.

The Mayflower Compact

Representing the first written laws in the New World, the Mayflower Compact is a very important part of American history and was signed on November 11, 1620 by all forty-one male passengers on the *Mayflower*. The purpose of the document was to establish governance in the colony. As it states:

> In the name of God, Amen. We, whose names are underwritten, the Loyal Subjects of our dread Sovereign Lord King James, by the Grace of God, of Great Britain, France, and Ireland, King, defender of the Faith, etc.:
>
> Having undertaken, for the Glory of God, and advancements of the Christian faith, and the honor of our King and Country, a voyage to plan the first colony in the Northern parts of Virginia; do by these presents, solemnly and mutually, in the presence of God, and one another; covenant and combine ourselves together into a civil body politic; for our better ordering, and preservation and furtherance of

the ends aforesaid; and by virtue hereof to enact, constitute, and frame, such just and equal laws, ordinances, acts, constitutions, and offices, from time to time, as shall be thought most meet and convenient for the general good of the colony; unto which we promise all due submission and obedience.

The Pilgrims had left England, risking their very lives in the voyage across the Atlantic, to establish a settlement in New England. Here they could raise their children based on the biblical principles they believed to be true, which were very different from those of the Church of England.

The Pilgrims left England behind them, but the tensions King James was experiencing in the Church of England did not dissipate as he supported efforts to maintain a broadly Catholic approach to worship. Protestants objected to the system of bishops and kneeling at the Eucharist. Tensions between Protestants and the king would continue after King James's son, Charles I, succeeded him in 1625. Charles I continued the practices within the Church of England that were contrary to Protestant beliefs, and many were forced to flee the country for the Netherlands or the New World.

Like his father before him, King Charles I believed he ruled by divine right and that he had been appointed by God to rule his kingdom. Divisions grew within the English government between the king and his aristocracy, known as "royalists," and those who believed the king should be accountable to his people, known as "parliamentarians."

The Thirty Years' War (1618–1648)

The Thirty Years' War was fought primarily in the area now known as Germany, but it spread over a very broad geographical area, including France, Spain, and Sweden. This war was one of the most destructive conflicts in European history and it resulted in a massive shift of power. The cause of the series of wars that made up the Thirty Years' War was primarily theological in nature, with Catholics fighting against Calvinists, Calvinists against Lutherans, and nationalists against imperialists. Casualties were enormous as entire regions were devastated. It is estimated that twenty-one million people were living in Germany in 1618, but by 1648 the number is estimated to be only thirteen million. Not even the plague was as destructive as the Thirty Years' War.

Witch-hunting was another trauma connected with this era, as hundreds of people were executed for the supposed practice of witchcraft. In the end, the Catholic Church lost a great deal of the power it had once held throughout Europe. While Sweden and France grew in power, the feudal system declined. The territorial split of Protestant and Catholic influence that resulted at the end of the war remains very much the same today.

While England did not directly participate in the Thirty Year's War, its inhabitants were not immune from the devastation of the theological wars and conflicts of the seventeenth century.

The English Civil War (1641–46)

The division between the king and Parliament escalated into war in 1641, which divided England both politically and theologically. For the most part, the parliamentarians were Puritans, while the royalists were Catholic. The Puritans were wanting the Church of England to adopt a more presbyterian structure, including abolishing the bishops and adopting a more Calvinistic doctrine. Civil war resulted in significant changes to the Church of England as well as a different relationship between the king and Parliament.

In 1643, the Anglican leaders met at Westminster Abbey and produced the Westminster Confession, which resulted in concessions to the Puritans including acknowledgment of the divine authorship and sufficiency of the Bible, predestination, and perseverance of the saints. In 1649, King Charles I was executed; Thomas Cromwell then acted as the dictator of England for ten years until his death in 1658; during that decade England operated as a commonwealth. In 1660, Charles I's son, Charles II, was crowned king, and the Church's movement toward Calvinism was reversed. The Westminster Confession was reversed in England and Scotland.

John Milton and John Bunyan

During Cromwell's rule of England, one of the country's greatest writers came into prominence, John Milton. Milton was a friend and defender of Cromwell, and he wrote *First Defense* in support of the Commonwealth of England under Cromwell. In 1667, impoverished and stricken with blindness, Milton wrote *Paradise Lost*, and in 1671, *Paradise*

Regained. Paradise Lost depicts the story of the fall of man, and the stated purpose of the book is to "justify the ways of God to men." Milton describes Satan's fall after his war against God; it is only by the grace of God that Satan was even able to lift his head out of the muck after his fall. Ultimately Satan expressed the sentiment that he would rather "reign in hell, then serve in heaven." Does the defiant attitude of Satan as portrayed in Milton's book mirror attitudes of any leaders in the twenty-first century?

Baptist preacher and writer John Bunyan penned *The Pilgrim's Progress* in 1678, which at one time was believed to be the most widely translated book in the English language aside from the Bible. Considered the most famous Christian allegory ever published, *The Pilgrim's Progress* tells the story of a man's journey from his hometown (the "City of Destruction") to that which is to come (the "Celestial City"). The main character, Christian, is burdened after becoming aware of his own sin after reading the "book in his hand," the Bible. Once considered a must-read, Bunyan's book no longer holds the place of prominence on believer's reading lists that it once did.

So among the weeds and thorns that seem to make up late-seventeenth-century England emerged two great authors whose work still speaks to us today. Not unlike other great works of literature, they are no longer held in great esteem or included in scholastic reading lists. This must change; we should challenge each other to become familiar with great works such as *Paradise Lost* and *The Pilgrim's Progress*.

The Church of England experienced significant changes during the course of the seventeenth century. After years of tension and fighting between Protestants and Catholics, including an outright civil war, the English Parliament issued the Toleration Act of 1689 granting relief to Protestants who did not conform to the Anglican Church of England. Under the Toleration Act, dissenters—referring to Baptists, Presbyterians, and Quakers—were allowed to worship in their own way. Excluded from the Act, however, were Catholics and Unitarians, meaning these groups were not free to practice their faith. Seventy years had passed since the Pilgrims left their homes seeking freedom to worship God in their own way, but in 1689 the legal right to do so was granted in England and extended to the British colonies across the Atlantic—except in Pennsylvania, where Catholics were allowed to practice their faith.

The Pilgrims established the second English settlement in America at

Plymouth during the winter of 1620, the first being Jamestown in 1607. The first governor of the Plymouth colony was John Carver, who had chartered the *Mayflower* and was the first to sign the Mayflower Compact. The Mayflower Compact, detailed earlier, is believed to be the world's first constitution. Upon Carver's death, William Bradford became the governor. Bradford first used the term *Pilgrims* in his journal *Of Plymouth Plantation*, where he borrows from Hebrews 11:13–16 in the following excerpt:

> So they lefte [that] goodly & pleasante citie, which had been ther resting place, nere 12 years; but they knew they were pilgrimes, & looked not much on these things; but lift up their eyes to ye heavens, their dearest cuntrie, and quieted their spirits.

The First Thanksgiving

The Plymouth colony struggled through a tough winter. By February 1621, 31 of the original 102 colonists had perished; by March there were only 47 survivors. The colony survived only with help from the Native Americans. Squanto was a Native American and a member of the Wampanoag tribe, led by Massasoit. He was taken back to England by Captain George Weymouth in 1605, where he was trained to be a guide and an interpreter. Squanto returned to the New England area in 1614 along with an expedition led by Captain John Smith. Trained as an interpreter, Squanto taught the Pilgrims how to catch eel and grow corn. The Wampanoag leader, Massasoit, who donated food to the Pilgrims' colony, provided additional help. In 1621 the grateful Pilgrims celebrated their first harvest along with ninety Native Americans over a three-day period.

The Pilgrims who settled at Plymouth in 1620 were Separatists. In 1628, Puritans from England established their own community, the Massachusetts Bay Colony, in the area now known as Boston.

Colonization of Canada

The English were planting settlements on the northern Atlantic coast of North America, and in Canada, the French had colonized "New France" in the late 1500s for Roman Catholic settlers. Catholic missionaries worked with the Huron tribe, which allied with the French against the Iroquois. While the French attempted to expose the Huron tribe to

Christianity, they inadvertently helped bring about the fall of the tribe by exposing them to diseases such as smallpox and by selling them alcohol.

Over a period of several years, the Huron tribe was greatly weakened by their exposure to the French, and they eventually fell to the Iroquois in 1649. The expansion of European Christian colonies in North America occurred at the expense of Native American lives. Sadly the story of Spain and Portugal's exploration and colonization of Central and South America did not end well for the indigenous peoples either.

Colonization of Central and South America

Portuguese explorer Christopher Columbus discovered the Americas in 1492 while sailing under commission to the Spanish crown, and Spanish and Portuguese exploration surged in the sixteenth century in Central and South America. Spanish explorer Balboa crossed Panama and reached the Pacific Ocean. Portuguese explorer Ferdinand Magellan sailed around the southern tip of South America and eventually around the world, although Magellan himself would die during the voyage.

During his voyage Magellan brought Christianity to each people group he encountered. Unfortunately, he was killed in April 1521 during the Battle of Mactan, in which forty-nine Spanish explorers faced 1,500 Native American warriors. But the accomplishments of Magellan's voyage are enormous; he was the first to circumnavigate the globe, to measure the distance around the earth, and to realize the need for an international date line.

The Conquistadors

The Americas contained inhabitants, an estimated total fifty-seven million people, at the time of Columbus's arrival—one-eighth of the world's population. In 1520 conquistador Herman Cortes conquered and brought down the Aztec tribe, which was based in Central America. A few years later Francisco Pizarro brought down the Incas, who lived in the Andes. A frequent practice was to enslave the conquered peoples, a practice of which the Church did not approve, but it could do nothing about.

Some protests were raised by clergy, including the first priest to be ordained in the "New World" in 1510, Bartolome de Las Casas, who had sailed with Columbus on his third voyage. De Las Casas believed the New World was made available to Spain solely for the purpose of converting the natives to Christianity, and that the indigenous people should not be enslaved or exploited. King Ferdinand II of Spain was outraged when he learned of the gross mistreatment of the natives by Spaniards, and he sought a solution. In 1537 Pope Paul III insisted that the Amerindians (natives of Central and South America) should not be enslaved, even if they were not Christian, but his proclamation had little effect.

There were some men who believed the Amerindians were capable of great things and they worked for reform in their treatment. Vasco de Quiroga, a Spanish priest, had been influenced by Thomas More's novel *Utopia*, which described a society of equality and happiness, and he set out to create such a society in Michoacan (located in central Mexico), where he was made a bishop in 1537. He set up communities in which schools, churches, and hospitals were built. Like the early Church practice in the book of Acts, all possessions were pooled together for the common good. The utopian ideals taught by de Quiroga endured for many years after his death in 1565.

Beginning in 1609, the Jesuits worked with the native peoples in South America to plant mission stations within the existing culture, as opposed to replacing existing culture. Over a forty-year period, thirty stations were developed, with each functioning as a small town. They were very successful. With the stations, each community worked as a giant monastery, including specific hours for work, prayer, and rest. Everyone attended mass each day, and children were taught about matters of faith, as well as to read and write.

Over the course of the sixteenth and seventeenth centuries, both Central and South America were colonized by the Spanish and Portuguese, and the natives were converted to Catholicism. *Colonization* may not be the appropriate term considering the brutality frequently associated with the expansion of Spain and Portugal into these new territories. Greed was the major driving force for their exploration and expansion, not the planting of Christian missions, although Catholic missions led by Jesuits were successful.

The violence related to European expansion into the New World was staggering; the Aztec and Inca empires were virtually erased. During the seventeenth century, European settlements in North America would grow, but there was a heavy price to be paid by the Native American tribes, which would ultimately be displaced by the European immigrants.

The Powhatan Confederacy and Jamestown

The 1607 Jamestown settlement occurred in an area inhabited by nine Algonquian tribes known as the Powhatan Confederacy. Clashes involving gunfire began almost immediately as the settlers of Jamestown arrived, and many deaths took place within the first two weeks. Over the next several years, hostilities between the Virginia Company of London and the Powhatan Confederacy occurred as the native Algonquian tribes tried to stop the growth of the new settlements by force. A time of peace began in 1614, brought about by the marriage of Pocahontas and Englishman John Rolfe while she lived in England, where she was baptized. This peaceful period ended shortly after her death in 1617 at the age of twenty-two. One of John Rolfe's motivations for marrying Pocahontas was to facilitate her personal salvation. It is a fact that the Virginia Company had a goal of converting natives to Christianity.

The settlers in the Plymouth colony had a different experience with Native Americans than did the settlers in Jamestown. Historians believe this was because the Plymouth settlement was small and did not appear to be a threat to Massasoit, the leader of the Wampanoag Confederacy. In fact, without Massasoit, it is doubtful the Plymouth Colony would have even survived the first winter of 1620. While the settlers in Plymouth will be remembered as "Pilgrims" who were seeking freedom of religion, the settlement in Jamestown had a much different purpose and was much larger. Thus, the Native Americans perceived the Europeans in Jamestown as a threat to their existence, and of course history proves that they were right to be concerned.

The Jamestown settlement was the result of the charter of the Virginia Company of London, drafted in cooperation with King James I in 1606 for the purpose of establishing colonies in North America. It was also an investment opportunity for wealthy English merchants. King James I had granted exclusive rights to them to settle in the Chesapeake Bay area of Virginia. The Plymouth branch was granted land in the New England area. The Company was not successful, however, and over time it offered increased incentives to motivate English people to travel to Virginia. A second charter of the Company was drafted in 1609, which resulted in a great many deaths, as only 60 of 214 colonists survived. A third charter sought to correct the financial woes of the Company and added Bermuda (frequently referred to as Virgineola) as part of Virginia. In addition to dealing with the financial woes of the Company, colonists were dealing with increasing hostilities with the Native Americans.

War eventually erupted between the Powhatans and the English settlers, including an attack on the settlers on April 18, 1622, in which 350 of 1,240 colonists were killed, with some outlying settlements wiped out entirely. The Virginia Company published an account of the attack and used it as justification for a "perpetual war without peace or truce…to root out from being any longer a people, so cursed a nation, ungrateful to all benefitte, and incapable of all goodness." As English colonies expanded, Native Americans would be forced to withdraw from their lands. Although the stated motive of bringing the message of Christ and the opportunity for a Christian education was honorable, the methods employed and the resulting elimination of the indigenous peoples represent a black mark on Christian history.

John Eliot: Missionary to Native Americans, and the First Printed Bible in North America

Despite the hostilities that grew as English colonists expanded their territory in New England, efforts were made to bring Christianity to the Native Americans, including the publication of the first printed Bible in America, a translation into the Natick dialect of Algonquin. John Eliot, who led a church in Roxbury, Massachusetts, prepared the translation. Eliot spent ten years working on it, including collaborating with eleven hundred "praying Indians" whom he helped form into fourteen self-governing communities, or towns. He completed the translation of the New Testament in 1661, and the complete Bible in 1663. Many people might be surprised to discover the first printed Bible in North America was not printed in English, but in Algonquin; however, in my mind nothing else could be more appropriate.

John Eliot was also responsible for the first political book published in North America, as well as the first book to be banned by a North American governmental unit. *The Christian Commonwealth,* or *The Civil Policy of the Rising Kingdom of Jesus Christ*, was published in the late 1640s, and it proposed a form of government similar to the one Moses had established with the Israelites in the desert. In his book, Eliot asserted that "Christ is the only right heir to the Crown of England." Eliot's proposal reminds me of God's advice to Samuel in 1 Samuel 8, when the Israelites asked God for a king, essentially rejecting Him as their king. God warned them of the consequences of having an earthly king rule over them, but they did not listen, and when God gave them a king, it did not work out well.

Philip Jacob Spener: "Father of Pietism"

Most of us are familiar with the word *pious*, which is frequently used in a negative light. In 1675, Philip Jacob Spener, a Lutheran clergyman, published *Pia Desideria, Pious Desires* as a response to what he believed was a trend of growing laziness and immorality within the Lutheran Church. As a new minister, Spener believed strongly in the biblical principle of the priesthood of believers, and he challenged his congregation to develop a relationship with Christ on a personal level and not be dependent upon the clergy for their faith. This did not sit well with the clergy of the day, who saw themselves as central figures to a believer's faith, not unlike the Catholic priests. Church leaders believed that individualism led to trouble (apparently Protestant leaders had adopted the leadership weaknesses of their Catholic peers), but Spener opposed this thinking, espousing that believers should have their own personal experience with God.

Taking lessons from the recent wars fought over differences in doctrine and Church liturgy, Spener sought to avoid conflict and instead taught that differences should be discussed in the spirit of charity. Believers needed to understand and cling to the essentials of Christ's words. The teachings of Spener caused such furor that he was forced to relocate from Frankfurt to Dresden and later to Berlin.

Although the clergy of the day felt threatened by Spener's teachings of reform, churches that adopted his teachings experienced improvement in the lives of their laypeople. Small group meetings were encouraged, and the Bible came alive to the believers. Churches in the current era can take a lesson from Spener's work.

America: "Quilt of Many Denominations"

From the sixteenth century forward, Europe, Russia, Great Britain, France, and Spain were nations that held differing views of Christianity. Catholicism, the Orthodox Church, Lutherans, Calvinists, Anglicans, Presbyterians, Anabaptists, Puritans, Separatists, and Baptists represent the diverse Christian beliefs of the day. These were usually associated with a geographical region or ruling body. The New World across the Atlantic would be no different. The Puritans (also known as Congregationalists) who settled in Massachusetts allowed only members of their particular churches to vote. In Virginia, the Anglican Church was dominant, and the birthplace of the Baptist Church in America was Rhode Island—first established in 1638. Of course we have already considered how the Catholic French colonized Canada, so North America, like Europe, had become a "patchwork quilt" of denominations in the sixteenth and seventeenth centuries, just waiting for something to bring them together. That something would be passionate revivals led by fiery preachers who were part of the first "Great Awakening."

The "Age of Enlightenment" and the First "Great Awakening"

The beginnings of the Age of Enlightenment can be traced to the seventeenth century, and they were associated with philosophers such as Francis Bacon, Baruch Spinoza, John Locke, Voltaire, and Isaac Newton. In Europe this era resulted in a focus on scientific methods that challenged traditional faith. During this time a shift took place away from a biblical perspective to one of a more humanistic nature; there is no debating the great works of literature, art, and advances in science that occurred during this period, but an unfortunate result of the advancement of human culture was the belief that people no longer needed God. It is interesting to compare Jewish history to the settlement of North America: Periods of blessings seem to cause people to fall away from God, not draw near to Him.

Perhaps the Church today is not that much different from the Church in the seventeenth and eighteenth centuries. Having experienced a time of great revival and growth, apathy and indifference soon set in. The late Christian musician and songwriter Rich Mullins once said that it disturbed him that fans could quote the words to his songs back to him, but they could not quote the Scriptures. Apparently the Church was facing apathy back in the early 1700s, as well.

One of the great preachers during the first "Great Awakening" was Jonathan Edwards. Edwards entered Yale College at the age of thirteen and began to pastor his first church in Northampton, Massachusetts, in 1729. The pastor who had preceded Edwards experienced several periods of "harvests" during his tenure—times when the spirituality of the community was evident and people devoted time to God, Bible study, and worship. Edwards prayed for such a harvest, as well, and he produced some of the greatest theological writings the world has ever seen. Surprisingly, Edwards was not a flamboyant preacher, and he was not known for using methods designed to elicit an emotional response, yet his messages did evoke strong emotional responses; people came from great distances to hear him speak.

Jonathan Edwards studied Calvinism and believed in the doctrine of election. However, he believed that God chooses whom He will and whom He will not. It was Edwards's prayer that everyone would be a member of the "elect," and he prayed about the gravity of sin in a person's life and the need to turn to God.

Wouldn't it be great if America experienced another "Great Awakening"? If believers across the country entered a passionate, deliberate period of deep Bible study and remembrance of their heritage? The Church of the Savior, Jesus Christ, needs to be united against its common foe.

One of the goals of this book is to introduce a new generation of believers to their Christian heritage, including Jonathan Edwards. Believers should be able to trace their history back to Christ, King David, Moses, Abraham, and Adam. The Bible states there is a second Adam (see 1 Corinthians 15:45–49), and this is Christ. Is it important that we are able to connect our heritage back to Christ? Can a knowledge of our Christian history strengthen our faith? Yes! Headlines continue to reflect the unmistakable fact that there is an ongoing war against Christianity, including the teaching of any Christian history.

The following is from an April 25, 2014, story pertaining to a challenge by the ACLU to an elective course offered at a high school in Mustang, Oklahoma. This is an excerpt from the actual posted article:

OKLAHOMA CITY (AP) —A high school curriculum supported by Hobby Lobby chain president Steve Green, billed as a way to teach archaeology, history and the arts through Bible stories, also tells students God is always there in times of trouble and that sinners must "suffer the consequences" of disobeying.

The Mustang School Board in suburban Oklahoma City voted this month to place the Museum of the Bible curriculum in its schools as an elective for a one-year trial using the Bible to explain key principles

116

in the arts and sciences. While the course does explain the inspiration behind famous works of art and holds a prism to historical events, it also endorses behavior for religious reasons and implies that bad things happen as a direct result of disregarding God's rules.

The Associated Press obtained a draft copy of the curriculum from the American Civil Liberties Union of Oklahoma, which got it from the school district. The ACLU and the Freedom From Religion Foundation say "using the curriculum raises constitutional issues and want the school district to reconsider."

After reading a headline like this, it is hard to believe that the first printed book in America was actually a psalter, printed in 1640 by Stephen Daye. He published seventeen hundred copies of *The Bay Psalm Book*.

My deep love of the history of the Church is now meeting up with my love of American history. Christianity was a major contributing factor in the discovery and settlement of much of the Americas, along with greed for gold and expansion of European powers. However, there can be no denying the significant role that faith in God and the Church played in the lives of the Founding Fathers of the United States of America.

11

One Nation under God

Christians living in the United States are facing an unexpected challenge in the twenty-first century in teaching our children that most of our Founding Fathers practiced the Christian faith. But we shouldn't be surprised that there are challenges to our heritage. All it takes is for one generation to forget or to discredit their history, and the enemy wins. The enemy of our heritage is the same enemy that lied to Eve in the Garden of Eden, the same enemy that killed the children in Egypt and Bethlehem, the same enemy that seeks to eliminate the Jewish people from existence.

Passing on the important teachings of their faith is of prime importance to the Jewish people; they have succeeded in doing so for over 3,400 years. One purpose of this book is to accomplish that very thing for American Christians, to revive and preserve our heritage for future generations.

This chapter will cover significant documented facts related to the role that Christianity has played in the lives of some of the Founding Fathers and in the history of our country.

This section includes frequent references to David Barton's website, www.wallbuilders.com. Kirk Cameron's documentary *Monumental* includes an interview with David Barton, as well as an examination of several of the historical documents held in David's collection. The mission and purpose of WallBuilders is outlined as follows:

> WallBuilders is an organization dedicated to presenting America's forgotten history and heroes, with an emphasis on the moral, religious, and constitutional foundation on which America was built —a foundation which, in recent years, has been seriously attacked and undermined. In accord with what was so accurately stated by George Washington, we believe that "the propitious [favorable] smiles of

heaven can never be expected on a nation which disregards the eternal rules of order and right which heaven itself has ordained."

We begin with a document referred to by some as the "birth certificate" of the United States of America: the Declaration of Independence. Below is an excerpt from WallBuilders containing an excellent overview of the ratification of this document:

On July 2, 1776, Congress voted to approve a complete separation from Great Britain. Two days afterwards – July 4th – the early draft of the Declaration of Independence was signed, albeit by only two individuals at that time: John Hancock, President of Congress, and Charles Thompson, Secretary of Congress. Four days later, on July 8, members of Congress took that document and read it aloud from the steps of Independence Hall, proclaiming it to the city of Philadelphia, after which the Liberty Bell was rung. The inscription around the top of that bell, Leviticus 25:10, was most appropriate for the occasion: "Proclaim liberty throughout the land and to all the inhabitants thereof."

To see the turmoil in other nations, their struggles and multiple revolutions, and yet to see the stability and blessings that we have here in America, we may ask how has this been achieved? What was the basis of American Independence? John Adams said, "The general principles on which the Fathers achieved independence were the general principles of Christianity." Perhaps the clearest identification of the spirit of the American Revolution was given by John Adams in a letter to Abigail the day after Congress approved the Declaration. He wrote her two letters on that day; the first was short and concise, jubilant that the Declaration had been approved. The second was much longer and more pensive, giving serious consideration to what had been done that day. Adams cautiously noted: "This day will be the most memorable epic in the history of America. I am apt to believe that it will be celebrated by succeeding generations as the great anniversary festival."

It is amazing that on the very day they approved the Declaration, Adams was already foreseeing that their actions would be celebrated by future generations. Adams contemplated whether it would be proper to hold such celebrations, but then concluded that the day should be commemorated —but in a particular manner and with a specific spirit. As he told Abigail: "It ought to be commemorated as the day of deliverance by solemn acts of devotion to God Almighty."

The Faith of John Adams

Below is an excerpt from a letter written by John Adams in 1813, reflecting a deep and loving faith in God:

For this whole period I have searched after truth by every means and by every opportunity in my power, and with a sincerity and impartiality, for which I can appeal to God, my adored Maker. My religion is founded on the love of God and my neighbor; on the hope of pardon for my offences, upon contrition; upon the duty as well as the necessity of supporting with patience the inevitable evils of life; in the duty of doing no wrong, but all the good I can, to the creation, of which I am but an infinitesimal part.

—*Letter from John Adams to Thomas Jefferson, December 25, 1813*

The Faith of George Washington

The history book used by my middle school teacher included a picture of a statue of General George Washington on bended knee in prayer at Valley Forge. This image left a lasting impression on—that such a powerful leader would turn to God for help during the desperate hours of battle. This generation has seen a great effort to remove references to the God of the Bible from our textbooks. What is the price the next generation will pay for this extremely biased and frequently untrue view of history? If there is any doubt of George Washington's faith, read the following excerpt of a letter written from George Washington to Thomas Nelson on August 20, 1778:

The Hand of providence has been so conspicuous in all this, that he must be worse than an infidel that lacks faith, and more than wicked, that has not gratitude enough to acknowledge his obligations.

—*George Washington*

The Center for Vision and Values includes the following depiction of George Washington's faith on its website, www.visionandvalues.org:

> One point, however, is not debatable: Washington strongly believed that Providence played a major role in creating and sustaining the United States. In public pronouncements as commander in chief and president, he repeatedly thanked God for directing and protecting Americans in their struggle to obtain independence and create a successful republic. Arguably, no president has stressed the role of Providence in the nation's history more than Washington.

The Aitken Bible

Consider the question: Has the United States Congress ever approved or endorsed a Bible for use in the United States? Would it surprise you to know the answer is yes? Until the War for Independence in 1776, all English language Bibles were printed and imported from overseas, as the license to publish the King James Bible was held by the Crown. On January 21, 1781, nine months before the British surrendered in Yorktown, Virginia, Robert Aitken presented a petition to Congress offering to print "a neat Edition of the Holy Scriptures for use of schools."

Congress appointed a committee to study the proposal, and it acted on September 12, 1782, by endorsing the project. Below is the actual text of the endorsement:

> Resolved, that the United States in Congress assembled highly approve the pious and laudable undertaking of Mr. Aitken, as subservient to the interest of religion, as well as an instance of the progress of arts in the country, and being satisfied from the above report of his care and accuracy in the execution of the work, they recommend this edition of the Bible to the inhabitants of the United States, and hereby authorize him to publish the Recommendation in the manner he shall think proper.   —*Cha. Thomson, Sec'ry*

Robert Aitken produced what is now believed to be one of the rarest books in the world, the *Bible of the American Revolution*. In 1783 George Washington wrote a letter to Robert Aitken commending him for his work.

The Constitution of the United States of America

Ratified by all states in 1789, the Constitution is the basis for government in the United States to this very day. I'm afraid that most of us would make Barney Fife (of *The Andy Griffith Show*) look like a genius when attempting to quote the Preamble to the Constitution, which is printed below:

> We the People of the United States, in Order to form a more perfect Union, establish Justice, insure domestic Tranquility, provide for the common defense, promote the general Welfare, and secure the Blessings of Liberty to ourselves and our Posterity, do ordain and establish this Constitution for the United States of America.

The Constitution contains seven articles followed by twenty-seven amendments (known as the Bill of Rights), the last being ratified on May 8, 1992. The First Amendment, which relates to the freedom of religion, is highly debated, and reads as follows:

> Congress shall make no law respecting an establishment of religion, or prohibiting the free exercise thereof; or abridging the freedom of speech, or of the press; or the right of the people peaceably to assemble, and to petition the Government for a redress of grievances.

On July 10, 1790, the House of Representatives voted to locate the Capitol on a ten-square-mile site chosen by President George Washington.

George Washington's Farewell Address

I am not familiar with every farewell speech given by past presidents of the United States of America, but the one given by the first president on September 19, 1796, laid an excellent foundation for those who would follow after him. The website of the Heritage Foundation has published this farewell address in its entirety, including its notes. Below are excerpts from the website detailing two points taken from the address:

> The general theme of the Farewell Address is the preservation of the Union as the core of American nationhood. Washington warned

against sectionalism as the destroyer of the common interest and national character. The ties of the Union and the Constitution that made the various parts one must be cherished as sacred. 'The name of American, which belongs to you, in your national capacity must always exalt the just pride of Patriotism, more than any appellation derived from local discriminations.

In a self-governing nation, a unifying public opinion requires the enlightenment of formal institutions of education and of civic education. The "great Pillars of human happiness" and the "firmest props of the duties of Men and citizens," he emphasized, were religion and morality. "Of all the dispositions and habits which lead to political prosperity, Religion and morality are indispensable supports."

Perhaps the most brilliant man ever to serve as president of the United States was the author of the Declaration of Independence, Thomas Jefferson. Regarding Thomas Jefferson, President John F. Kennedy once remarked while hosting a dinner for American Nobel Prize winners:

I think that this is the most extraordinary collection of talent, of human knowledge, that has ever been gathered together at the White House, with the possible exception of when Thomas Jefferson dined alone.

Thomas Jefferson's personal faith is a matter of much debate, but documents do support the fact that he was no atheist. He wrote books expressing his admiration for the teachings of Jesus of Nazareth. The website www.monticello.org provides the following quotes:

1802 January 1. (Jefferson to the Baptist Association of Danbury, Connecticut). "Believing with you that religion is a matter which lies solely between Man & his God, that he owes account to none other for his faith or his worship, that the legitimate powers of government reach actions only, & not opinions, I contemplate with sovereign reverence that act of the whole American people which declared that their legislature should 'make no law respecting an establishment of religion, or prohibiting the free exercise thereof,' thus building a wall of separation between Church & State."

1803 April 21. (Jefferson to Benjamin Rush). "To the corruptions of Christianity I am indeed, opposed; but not to the genuine precepts of Jesus himself. I am a Christian, in the only sense in which he wished any one to be; sincerely attached to his doctrines, in preference to all others; ascribing to himself every human excellence; and believing he never claimed any other."

These statements include the historically significant mention of "a wall of separation between Church & State." One wonders if Thomas Jefferson would have ever uttered those famous (or infamous?) words had he known they would be used to expel God from American classrooms two hundred years later.

Quotes from Other Famous Americans

Young man, my advice to you is that you cultivate an acquaintance with and firm belief in the Holy Scriptures, for this is your certain interest. I think Christ's system of morals and religion, as He left them for us, the best the world ever saw or is likely to see.

—Benjamin Franklin

If we abide by the principles taught in the Bible, our country will go on prospering and to prosper; but, if we and our prosperity neglect its instructions and authority, no man can tell how sudden a catastrophe may overwhelm us and bury all our glory in profound obscurity. The Bible is the book of all others for lawyers as well as divines, and I pity the man who cannot find in it a rich supply of thought and rule of conduct. I believe Jesus Christ to be the Son of God. The miracles which He establish in my mind His personal authority and render it proper for me to believe what He asserts.   *—Daniel Webster*

The following information about John Wesley, William Wilberforce, and John Newton has been included in this chapter, as their contributions to our American and Christian heritage during this time period are significant.

"The World Is My Parish"

On May 24, 1738, Anglican priest John Wesley, who previously felt he lacked a "saving faith," had a life-changing experience. While listening to someone read *Luther's Preface to the Epistle of Romans*, he began to feel his heart warming, and he later wrote in his journal:

> ...I felt I did trust in Christ, Christ alone for salvation, and an assurance was given me that he had taken away my sins, even mine, and saved me from the law of sin and death.

Wesley at first worked with evangelist George Whitefield, but he eventually parted from him and organized his followers into societies. When those societies became too large, classes were formed, each having eleven members and a leader. While organizing these believers, Wesley continued to serve as an Anglican priest; when his bishop objected, Wesley retorted, "The world is my parish." John Wesley's brother Charles, who was also an Anglican priest, joined him in his efforts. Charles Wesley is credited for writing over 6,500 hymns, including "O for a Thousand Tongues to Sing" and "Hark, the Herald Angels Sing." Despite the tremendous increase in the followers of John Wesley's "methods," he never left the Church of England.

Critics of Wesley had called his followers "Methodists" at one time; they were proud of that name and adopted it as their own. In 2014 it is estimated that there are about thirty million Methodists worldwide.

"Amazing Grace"

Many men of faith challenged the horrible practice of slavery and the powerful and wealthy industry that benefited from it. In England, two of those men were William Wilberforce and John Newton. John Newton was at first involved with the slave trade, but he came under conviction on May 10, 1748, and became a prominent supporter of abolition a few years later. In 1764 Newton became an Anglican priest.

In 1788 Newton broke his silence related to his involvement in the slave trade and published the pamphlet *Thoughts Upon the Slave Trade*, which detailed the terrible conditions of the slave ships. It also included an apology. A copy of the pamphlet was sent to every member of Parliament.

It was during his years as a priest that Newton met William Wilberforce, who was the leader of the abolition movement in Parliament.

John Newton was a talented songwriter, and he is credited with writing the words to *Faith's Review and Expectation,* best known by its first verse of "Amazing Grace." This song was first published in 1779.

William Wilberforce became a member of Parliament in 1784. In 1785 he experienced a spiritual conversion and became an evangelical Christian. From his years of effort a bill abolishing slavery was eventually passed in 1833, just weeks after his death. The selfless work of Wilberforce was acknowledged during the passing of the *Bill for the Abolition of Slavery.*

The struggle to end slavery in the United States up to the time of the beginning of the Civil War in 1861 is well documented. We will now focus on the faith of great men who led this country during that time of great division.

Richard Allen: "Black Founding Father"

Born into slavery on February 14, 1760, Richard Allen converted to Methodism in 1787, taught himself to read and write, and was able to buy his own freedom in 1783. In 1799 he became the first African American to be ordained in the ministry of the Methodist-Episcopal Church. In 1816 he founded the first national black church in the United States, the African Methodist Episcopal Church (AME).

Allen also founded the Free Produce Society, whose members would only purchase products from non-slave labor, and he fought for an end to slavery. In his 2008 biography of Richard Allen, author Richard Newman suggested that Allen be referred to as the "black founding father." The Reverend Richard Allen was truly a great man who left a remarkable legacy that eventually influenced Frederick Douglass and Dr. Martin Luther King Jr.

"The Star-Spangled Banner"

Francis Scott Key wrote the words to "The Star-Spangled Banner" in 1814, during the War of 1812. Key wrote a poem based on witnessing the bombardment of Fort McHenry while on board a British ship. His poem was titled "Defense of Fort McHenry," which contained the words to what was to become our national anthem. Music was put with the words, and the song was first performed on October 19, 1814; it was published as "The Star-Spangled Banner" shortly afterward. It was a popular song during the Civil War as people turned to music to express their ideals and feelings for the flag and the values it represented. The song includes the phrase "And this be our motto: 'In God is our Trust.'"

Andrew Jackson

When I was young, my parents took our family to visit the Hermitage, the home of Andrew Jackson located near Nashville, Tennessee. Jackson is also known as "Old Hickory," and he won many battles, including leading 5,000 troops to defeat 7,500 British soldiers in the Battle of New Orleans. The Democratic Party can thank Andrew Jackson for the symbol of the jackass, a nickname given to Jackson by his opponent during the 1828 election, which Jackson won by a landslide. Jackson was a two-term president, was known as the "people's president," and was the founder of the Democratic Party. Unfortunately, President Jackson also presided over very poor treatment practices of Native Americans, including the passage of the Indian Removal Act of 1830 by the twenty-first Congress, which led to the "Trail of Tears."

The Trail of Tears

The period of the "Trail of Tears" covers ten years and the removal of approximately seventy thousand Indians from their homelands to an area west of the Mississippi thought to have little value. Unfortunately for the Native Americans, that changed in 1906, and they were forced to move again. Because I live in Tennessee, I am more familiar with the Cherokee tribe, whose move resulted in the deaths of over four thousand Native Americans from starvation, exposure, or disease. After the passage of the Indian Removal Act, Jackson gave a speech to Congress that included the following excerpt:

> It will separate the Indians from immediate contact with settlements of whites; enable them to pursue happiness in their own way and under their own rude institutions; will retard the progress of decay, which is lessening their numbers, and perhaps cause them gradually, under the protection of the government and through the influences of

good counsels, to cast off their savage habits and become an interesting, civilized, and Christian community. *—Andrew Jackson, 1830*

We should examine the living conditions of Native Americans today. These people were forced to give up their land in the United States and were moved to terrain with very poor conditions, where they still live to this day. Have they thrived under the "protection of the government"? Maybe this is a lesson to future generations regarding living under the absolute oversight of the federal government.

The Indian Removal Act of 1830 is a black mark on the career of a great man, President Andrew Jackson, and a black mark on the Christians of the day who supported it.

History that matters is not always a history of encouragement, but it is part of who we are.

12

A House Divided

As mentioned in the previous chapter, greed was one of the reasons for the exploration of the Americas; greed also prevented the removal of a cancer from the formation of the United States. That cancer was slavery. Several of the Founding Fathers wanted the practice to be made illegal and identified this desire in the Declaration of Independence as such, but they gave in to the wishes of other leaders whose financial prosperity relied heavily on the practice in order to obtain full support. Great wealth was accumulated at the expense of the enslavement of others in England and the United States. We've already considered the work of Reverend Richard Allen; next we will learn about a person whom Allen influenced, Frederick Douglass.

Frederick Douglass

In 1845 former slave Frederick Douglass authored *Narrative of the Life of Frederick Douglass, an American Slave, Written by Himself*. Douglass also published his own newspaper, *The North Star*, as well as three autobiographies. In addition to being a strong leader in the abolitionist movement, he was a supporter of women's rights. Obviously he had a different perspective of Christianity in the United States as indicated by the following quote:

> I am filled with unutterable loathing when I contemplate the religious pomp and show, together with the horrible inconsistencies, which every where surround me. We have men-stealers for ministers, women-whippers for missionaries, and cradle-plunderers for church members. The man who wields the blood-clotted cowskin during the week fills the pulpit on Sunday, and claims to be a minister of the meek and lowly Jesus.... The slave auctioneer's bell and the church-

going bell chime in with each other, and the bitter cries of the heart-broken slave are drowned in the religious shouts of his pious master. Revivals of religion and revivals in the slave-trade go hand in hand together. The slave prison and the church stand near each other. The clanking of fetters and the rattling of chains in the prison, and the pious psalm and solemn prayer in the church, may be heard at the same time.

Douglass clearly saw the hypocrisy in the country with respect to Christians' tolerance of slavery, primarily in the South. It is clear, though, that Frederick Douglass had his own understanding of what Christianity should be, as reflected in the following words of his:

Though for weeks I was a poor broken-hearted mourner traveling through doubts and fears, I finally found my burden lightened, and my heart relieved. I loved all mankind, slaveholders not excepted, though I abhorred slavery more than ever. I saw the world in a new light and my great concern was to have everybody converted. My desire to learn increased, and especially did I want a thorough acquaintance with the contents of the Bible.   —*Frederick Douglass*

The Faith of Abraham Lincoln

Abraham Lincoln's faith is sometimes questioned by those seeking to prove that it played little to no role in his decisions. On March 30, 1863, however, Lincoln issued the following proclamation to establish a National Day of Fasting and Prayer:

It is the duty of nations as well as of men to own their dependence upon the overruling power of God, and to confess their sins and transgressions in humble sorrow, yet with assured hope that genuine repentance will lead to mercy and pardon, and to recognize the sublime truth, announced in Holy Scripture, and proven by all history, that those nations only are blessed whose God is the Lord. And, insomuch (sic) as we know that by His divine law nations, like individuals, are subjected to punishments and chastisement in this world, may we not justly fear that the awful calamity of civil war which now desolates the land may be but a punishment inflicted upon us for our presumptuous sins, to the needful end of our national reformation as a whole people? We have been the recipients of the choicest bounties of Heaven; we have been preserved these many years in peace and prosperity; we have grown in numbers, wealth and power as no other nation has ever grown. But we have forgotten God. We have forgotten the gracious hand which has preserved us in peace and multiplied and enriched and strengthened us, and we have vainly imagined, in the deceitfulness of our hearts, that all these blessings were produced by some superior wisdom and virtue of our own. Intoxicated with unbroken success, we have become too self-sufficient to feel the necessity of redeeming and preserving grace, too proud to pray to the God that made us. It behooves us, then, to humble ourselves before the offended power, to confess our national sins and to pray for clemency and forgiveness.

"A House Divided Against Itself Cannot Stand"

On June 16, 1858, Lincoln delivered a famous speech to more than a thousand Republican delegates in Springfield, Illinois, at the Republican State Convention. In speaking about the failed policy regarding slavery at the time and the possibility of a coming crisis, he quoted Jesus (as recorded in Matthew, Mark, and Luke), that "a house divided against itself cannot stand." Lincoln was his party's nomination for the Senate, and in 1860 he was his party's nomination for president. Lincoln won the election, but before his inauguration in March 1861, seven Southern states had seceded from the Union. On April 12, 1861, Fort Sumter in Charleston, South Carolina was fired upon and the Civil War began.

The Great Revival

During the period of the Civil War, there were many revivals, but one was known as the "Great Revival." It began in the fall of 1863 and lasted through the summer of 1864. It is estimated that 100,000 Confederate troops and between 100,000 and 200,000 Union troops came to Christ during the Civil War.

According to J. William Jones, Confederate Chaplain and author of one of the best documentaries of the Great Revival, virtually every Confederate brigade was affected—and approximately ten percent of the soldiers in the Army of Northern Virginia accepted Christ. Night after night troops participated in prayer meetings, worshipped, and listened to ministers proclaim the good news. Virtually every gathering ended with soldiers coming forward to accept Christ or receive prayer. When a pond or river was nearby, the soldiers would frequently step forward for baptisms—regardless of how cold the weather was.

During the revival, Jones told of how Confederate soldiers would form "reading clubs," in which soldiers would pass around a well-worn Bible, sharing the Gospel. Always hungry for scarce Testaments and religious tracts, the soldiers would see Jones approaching camp and cry out "Yonder comes the Bible and Tract man!" and run up to him and beg for Bibles and Testaments "as if they were gold guineas for free distribution." Jones would quickly exhaust his supply of reading material, and sadly have to turn away most of the men. "I have never seen more diligent Bible-readers than we had in the Army of Northern Virginia."

The U.S. Christian Commission

In stark contrast to the role the executive branch of the United States government was playing in the military of the current time, Lincoln believed faith would play a key role in stabilizing the army, and he supported the organization of the U.S. Christian Commission. The Christian Commission was made up of civilians who lived near military camps and provided support to the soldiers, such as the giving of Bibles and tracts as well as medical care. They were also given the support and freedom to spread the gospel.

By the time General Robert E. Lee surrendered to General Ulysses S. Grant at the Appomattox Courthouse on April 9, 1865, it is estimated that 620,000 people had died, with more recent estimates as high as 850,000 (according to www.civilwar.org), but Lincoln's goal to preserve the Union was achieved. Was it an answered prayer that the United States would persevere? Could the nation heal economically, militarily, or spiritually? Lincoln paid for the unity of the nation with his life, along with countless others, to preserve the ideal of the United States, and the process of removing a great cancer in the form of slavery had begun.

George Washington Carver

I love to think of nature as an unlimited broadcasting station, through which God speaks to us every hour, if we will only tune in.

Believed to be born in 1862, although there is no record of his birth to confirm this, George Washington Carver was the son of a slave. After the Civil War, George's former owner, Moses Carver, loved and cared for him and his brother. George and his brother assumed the last name of the Carvers and lived with them after the war. Moses Carver was a successful farmer who understood both animals and crops. George spent hours in the garden and learned a great deal about plants.

While attending school, he boarded with a couple who took him to church and encouraged him to read his Bible. George Washington Carver continued to improve his education over the years, which was very difficult during that time period, and in the fall of 1895 he was offered a teaching position at the Tuskegee Institute in Tuskegee, Alabama. Professor Carver proved to be a tenderhearted mentor who cared very much for his students. He was a devout Christian who believed in God, and he told his students that the more they knew about plants and the natural world, the more they would know about their Creator. In 1907 he was asked to teach a Bible study on Sunday nights. Attendance grew from about fifty boys in the first session, to more than a hundred boys just three months later.

Carver's great contributions to science are well-documented, including the multiple uses he came up with for the peanut. In January 1921, he was retained by the United Peanut Growers Association as an expert witness, and he testified before Congress on protecting the domestic peanut from imports. His performance was effective, and he showed the public that an intelligent, educated black person, a professor, could greatly contribute to society.

In June 1942, Carver visited Henry Ford in Dearborn, Michigan, and toured the Ford Motor Company's facilities with him. The two became very close during their time together, and Ford dedicated the Carver Museum in November 1941. Carver died on January 5, 1943, but his legacy in Tuskegee remains strong in the school of veterinary medicine, which has trained 70 percent of the black veterinarians in America.

Sergeant Alvin C. York

With respect to World War I, our Christian heritage is well-represented by Sergeant Alvin C. York. Raised in the hills of Tennessee, York was known to be an excellent marksman, but he was also known for drinking and his temper. His salvation, which took place on New Year's Eve of 1914, was an answer to his mother's prayer. She was very concerned for her rowdy, violent son. York is remembered for his significant role in capturing 132 German prisoners on October 8, 1918, for which he was awarded the Congressional Medal of Honor.

The film based on his life, *Sergeant York*, starring Gary Cooper, was the highest grossing movie of 1941. York's personal convictions are reflected in the following quote:

> If this country fails, it will fail from within. I think we've just got to go back to the old time religion, shouting as though the world is on fire. Maybe people will realize we've gotten onto some wrong roads and return to the old paths.

World War II

After World War I, a great evil manifested itself in Germany, but Americans again ignored this evil as it grew. This ignorance reminds me of the *Lord of the Rings* trilogy, in which evil, when left unchecked, continues to grow until it either consumes a person, or a person overcomes it. This evil took the form of a man named Adolf Hitler and the nightmare he helped to create.

Adolf Hitler was elected chancellor of Germany in 1933. His forces invaded Poland in 1939—the same year he was nominated for the Nobel Peace Prize—resulting in declarations of war from both England and France. In June 1941 Hitler invaded Russia, and still the United States stood by waiting. Finally, on December 7, 1941, the Japanese sneak attack on Pearl Harbor resulted in the United States' getting involved in the war, but by then Hitler's forces were very strong in Europe.

When the Allied forces defeated Germany, what they discovered in the concentration camps was horrifying. The Nazis had murdered approximately six million Jews as Hitler attempted to commit a complete genocide of the Jewish race. It is estimated that between sixty and eighty-five million people died during World War II. The Holocaust is evidence of the great evil that man is able to commit in his disobedience of God.

Is another Holocaust possible? I believe the Holocaust of our generation is actually "abortion on demand," which has resulted in the deaths of nearly fifty-seven million babies—as of the writing of this book in the summer of 2014—in the United States since the *Roe versus Wade* decision in 1973. (See www.numberofabortions.com for further details.) I know this is an issue that divides the nation, as did slavery and our involvement in World War II, but the numbers are staggering for this mostly unregulated "business."

The Pledge of Allegiance

The "Pledge to the Flag" was originally written by Francis Bellamy in 1892, was modified in 1923, and was adopted by Congress in 1942. The words "under God" were added at the request of President Dwight D. Eisenhower in 1954. The following is the story of how President Eisenhower was inspired to request that those words be added to the pledge.

"In Scotland," Rev. George Docherly stated, "the people said 'God save the king/queen.'" That was the opening statement made to an Associated Pressman Dan Lawrence regarding the pastor's influence in to the addition of "one nation under God" to the Pledge of Allegiance to the American flag. Rev. Docherly, former pastor of Washington's New York Avenue Presbyterian Church, was instrumental in having that phrase inserted into the Pledge fifty years ago. On February 7, 1954, Pastor Docherly delivered a sermon that included the thought that "something is missing from the Pledge—the characteristic definitive factor in the American way of life." In attendance at that service was President Dwight Eisenhower. The Scottish pastor decided to take that opportunity to point out that God wasn't in the Pledge of Allegiance! A transcript of the sermon was reprinted in the Congressional Record. The new phrase received official recognition by Congress in an Act approved June 22, 1954 and the pastor's hope that the words honoring God would be added to the Pledge was fulfilled. For fifty years people have been saying "one nation under God" when they say the pledge to the flag.

It is significant that President Eisenhower said at that time, "In this way we are reaffirming the transcendence of religious faith in America's heritage and future; in this way we shall constantly strengthen those spiritual weapons which forever will be our country's most powerful resource in peace and war."

We remember that Patrick Henry said, "Righteousness alone can exalt (the people) as a nation.... It cannot be emphasized too strongly or too often that this great nation was founded, not by religionists, but by Christians; not on religions, but on the Gospel of Jesus Christ." How appropriate, then, it is to honor God whose providential care brought about "one nation under God." We think about that every time we pledge allegiance to the flag of the United States of America.

—*www.americanchristianhistory.com*

The words of President Eisenhower are inspiring to me even as I write this sentence. He was a truly great leader who spoke the truth about our nation's heritage. Recently, there have been efforts to have the words "under God" removed from the Pledge; pray that these efforts are not successful.

Billy Graham

When considering the great evangelists of the twentieth century, the first name that comes to mind is the Reverend Billy Graham. Countless believers have come forward to accept Christ at his revivals. I always think of him whenever I hear the phrase, "the Bible says," or the hymn "Just As I Am." These are always pleasant memories. Consider that no serious scandal that I am aware of has ever rocked his ministry—rare in this day and age.

His wife, Ruth, who died in June 2007 at the age of eighty-seven, was an example of a godly wife for women everywhere. Mrs. Graham also was deeply involved in ministries of her own, and she authored, or coauthored, fourteen books. Mrs. Graham was a strong supporter of her husband's in-credible ministry, as well; Billy and Ruth Graham were jointly awarded the Congressional Gold Medal in 1996.

The Reverend Billy Graham was born on November 7, 1918, in Charlotte, North Carolina, and he has dedicated his entire life to the spread of the gospel of Christ. During the most active years of his worldwide ministry, the mid-1940s through 1992, when he was diagnosed with Parkinson's disease, it is estimated that approximately 3.2 million responded to his message to "accept Christ as your Savior." It is estimated that his lifelong radio and television audience has topped 2.2 billion. He was close friends with Presidents Dwight D. Eisenhower, Lyndon Johnson, and Richard Nixon. In 1957, he led a joint revival in New York City with Dr. Martin Luther King Jr.

The 1991 biography of Billy Graham entitled *A Prophet with Honor: The Billy Graham Story*, by William Martin, represents an unbiased study of "America's pastor." Martin openly admitted in his book that he was surprised, though very appreciative, when Graham approached him about writing a book about his life, ministry, and niche in history. Graham told Martin that there would be no "conditions" to the book, that he was to write it as he saw fit. Graham didn't even have to read it, nor would any of Graham's organizations participate in any income derived from the book. I highly recommend that you read Martin's book for an honest and well-researched view of Billy Graham's ministry.

Dr. Martin Luther King Jr.

Dr. Martin Luther King Jr. was born on January 15, 1929; his legal name given at birth was Michael King, the same as his father. His father changed both of their names to Martin Luther, in honor of the German reformer, after attending the 1934 First Baptist World Alliance, held in Berlin. King received his undergraduate degree from Morehouse College in 1948, and he completed his doctoral studies in systematic theology and received his Ph.D. on June 5, 1955. King married Coretta Scott in 1953; together they had four children: Yolanda Denise King, who died in 2007, Martin Luther King III, Dexter Scott King, and Bernice Albertine King.

On August 28, 1963, Dr. King delivered his famous "I Have a Dream" speech while speaking to a massive crowd during the March on Washington for Jobs and Freedom.

His many awards include the Nobel Peace Prize, awarded in 1964; the Presidential Medal of Freedom, awarded in 1977; and the Congressional Gold Medal, awarded in 2004. Describing the contributions made by Dr. King to the advancement of civil rights for African Americans both during and after his lifetime, would fill volumes. He was a proponent of non-violent protests. In a 1967 letter, written from a jail in Birmingham, Alabama, King wrote:

> Before I was a civil rights leader, I was a preacher of the Gospel. This was my first calling and it still remains my greatest commitment. You know, actually all that I do in civil rights I do because I consider it a part of my ministry. I have no other ambitions in life but to achieve excellence in the Christian ministry. I don't plan to run for any political office. I don't plan to do anything but remain a preacher. And what I'm doing in this struggle, along with many others, grows out of my feeling that the preacher must be concerned about the whole man.
>
> —*Dr. Martin Luther King Jr., 1967*

Another quote from Dr. King, which I take to heart as every believer should, states, "The ultimate measure of a man is not where he stands in moments of comfort and convenience, but where he stands at times of challenge and controversy."

The world changed on April 4, 1968, when Martin Luther King Jr. was murdered in Memphis, Tennessee. He had gone to that city to support black sanitary works employees during their strike. According to the Reverend Jesse Jackson, who was present that day, King's last words were spoken to musician Ben Branch: "Ben, make sure you play 'Take My Hand, Precious Lord' in the meeting tonight. Play it real pretty."

Dr. King's legacy, like those of the other courageous men and women mentioned in this book, changed the world and must be preserved for generations to come.

The Chicago Statement on Biblical Inerrancy

In the fall of 1978, three hundred noted evangelical scholars met at an international summit conference held at the Hyatt-Regency O'Hare in Chicago. During the conference, they drafted the Chicago Statement on Biblical Inerrancy. This statement was important as it came at a time when the authority of the Bible was being seriously challenged. Below is an excerpt from the statement:

A Short Statement

1. God, who is Himself Truth and speaks truth only, has inspired Holy Scripture in order thereby to reveal Himself to lost mankind through Jesus Christ as Creator and Lord, Redeemer and Judge. Holy Scripture is God's witness to Himself.

2. Holy Scripture, being God's own Word, written by men prepared and superintended by His Spirit, is of infallible divine authority in all matters upon which it touches: it is to be believed, as God's instruction, in all that it affirms: obeyed, as God's command, in all that it requires; embraced, as God's pledge, in all that it promises.

3. The Holy Spirit, Scripture's divine Author, both authenticates it to us by His inward witness and opens our minds to understand its meaning.

4. Being wholly and verbally God-given, Scripture is without error or fault in all its teaching, no less in what it states about God's acts in creation, about the events of world history, and about its own literary origins under God, than in its witness to God's saving grace in individual lives.

5. The authority of Scripture is inescapably impaired if this total divine inerrancy is in any way limited or disregarded, or made relative to a view of truth contrary to the Bible's own; and such lapses bring serious loss to both the individual and the Church.

Ronald Reagan

Ronald Reagan began his two-term presidency of the United States in January 1981. He openly expressed his belief in God, and for the most part, his support of biblical values in his self-prepared inauguration speech: "In this present crisis, government is not the solution to our problems; government is the problem."

Reagan believed strongly in prayer in the public schools as well as in states' rights.

Unfortunately, in the last two decades we've experienced an onslaught of such twisted logic that if Alice were visiting America, she might think she'd never left Wonderland. We're told that it somehow violates the rights of others to permit students in school who desire to pray to do so. Clearly this infringes on the freedom of those who choose to pray, the freedom taken for granted since the time of our Founding Fathers. —*Ronald Reagan, September 25, 1982*

In March 1984, the Senate voted down a constitutional amendment protecting voluntary prayer in public schools. In speaking of this vote, Reagan made the following statement:

To prevent those who believe in God from expressing their faith is an outrage... The relentless drive to eliminate God from our schools... should be stopped. —*Ronald Reagan, February 25, 1984*

President Reagan made a stand for his Christian values. Of course, like all presidents, he made mistakes and was not perfect. In my mind, however, Reagan represents a marker in our Christian American heritage.

Promise Keepers' "Stand in the Gap" Gathering in Washington, DC

On October 4, 1997, over one million men traveled to our nation's capital to pray for our nation and our country's families. The stated purpose of this gathering was "to gather a diverse multitude of men in the name of Jesus Christ, to confess personal and collective sin so that we may present to the Lord, godly men on their knees in humility, then on their feet in unity, reconciled and poised for revival and spiritual awakening."

I was there; the experience was supernatural, and I was a skeptic. Park Rangers at the event told me that they had never seen a crowd like this one before, and there could be no doubt that the attendance was in excess of one million people. Arial photographs of the event do not dispute the massive outpouring of men. I'll never forget meeting a man sitting next to me, who had flown a small private plane there from a western state; we were immediately like brothers. Can a gathering like this happen again in our nation's capital? I pray that it does.

If there is any one lesson that we should take from this chapter, it is that our Christian American heritage is significant, very relevant, and a work in process. What a tragedy it would be to fail to pass it on to our children. If we are keeping up with world events, no doubt we are noticing that those who fail to protect their heritage are finding it challenged, rewritten, and even removed from the records altogether.

Our history matters, and we must do what is necessary to protect it.

13

The British Invasion

Most of us are familiar with the "British invasion" of the early 1960s by the Dave Clark Five, the Beatles, the Rolling Stones, and many other British bands. The Beatles were often referred to as the "Fab Four," and their music and lyrics are widely studied to this day. But there is another "British invasion" that occurred prior to the Beatles' arrival in the United States; although it was spread over several years, it was led by my Christian "Fab Four" of Jane Austen, Charles Dickens, C. S. Lewis, and J.R.R. Tolkien.

Some of the most successful movies in recent years have been based on books written by this "Fab Four," including *Pride and Prejudice*, *A Christmas Carol*, *The Chronicles of Narnia*, and *The Lord of the Rings*. With the exception of C. S. Lewis, there seems to be little knowledge about the Christian faith of these authors, which is sad (for believers). We can be encouraged that these authors, considered by many to be among the greatest who ever lived, were people of deep faith in Christ, and that they made a significant contribution to our Christian heritage.

Jane Austen

When it comes to Jane Austen, I must confess that, as a male, I share the views of Tom Hank's character in the 1998 movie *You've Got Mail*. Researching this chapter has caused me to become a great admirer of Ms. Austen's work and faith. In addition to *Pride and Prejudice*, her works include *Sense and Sensibility*, *Emma*, and *Mansfield Park*—all published between 1811 and 1815. Ms. Austen died in 1817, at the age of forty-one. Two additional completed works were published after her death, *Northanger Abbey* and *Persuasion*.

Jane Austen was born on December 16, 1775; her father was the Reverend George Austen, of the Steventon Rectory, and her mother was Cassandra Austen. Regarding the Christian faith of Jane Austen, the following is an excerpt of a letter written on November 18, 1814, to her niece Fanny Knight, regarding Knight's fiancé:

> ...from the danger of his becoming even Evangelical, I cannot admit that I am by no means convinced that we ought not all to be Evangelicals, & am at least persuaded that they who are so from Reason and Feeling, must be happiest & safest. Do not be frightened from the connection by your Brothers having most wit. Wisdom is better than Wit, & in the long run will certainly have the laugh on her side; & don't be frightened by the idea of his acting more strictly up to the precepts of the New Testament than others.

Author Peter Leithart wrote of Ms. Austen's works in his 2004 book, *Miniatures and Morals: The Christian Novels of Jane Austen*. Mr. Leithart's book analyzed the characters and themes of Austen's major works, and it is considered an excellent introduction for both students and those seeking a deeper appreciation of her books.

Charles Dickens

One of my favorite lines from any book, excluding the Bible, is from *A Christmas Carol*, when the Ghost of Christmas Present responds to Ebenezer Scrooge regarding his insensitive remarks about the deaths of those hurting ultimately helping to reduce the "surplus population": "It may be, that in the sight of Heaven you are more worthless and less fit to live than millions like this poor man's child." In the movie version, starring George C. Scott, this scene is especially well done. The author's message is clear in both the movie and the book: Scrooge is starting to realize his ignorance and hypocrisy, and the Ghost of Christmas Present hammers home the point that God's standards are different from mankind's. We must be clear: Charles Dickens was a believer in the God he mentions in *A Christmas Carol*.

Charles Dickens was born on February 7, 1812, and he died on June 9, 1870, at the age of fifty-eight. He is considered by many to be the greatest

English writer of the nineteenth century. In addition to *A Christmas Carol*, published in 1843, his great works include *The Adventures of Oliver Twist*, *David Copperfield, Bleak House, Hard Times: for These Times, A Tale of Two Cities,* and *Great Expectations*. Dickens is remembered for the social commentary in his books, as well as for speaking out against the social injustices of the day. But for me, *A Christmas Carol* could have been another book in the Bible; I never fail to learn some new lesson every time I watch the movie or read the book. Most people remember the character of Tiny Tim and the phrase "God bless us, every one," but there are many more lessons to be gleaned from the story.

The Ghost of Christmas Past reminds Scrooge of the day his fiancée broke off their engagement, because "another idol had replaced her." The point I so admire Dickens for making in this encounter is that of her strength in releasing him and then wishing him joy in the life he has chosen. Later he sees images of her with the children she has with her husband, and he ponders the fact that they could have been his own. This is brilliant; imagine coming face-to-face with the consequences of your poor decisions. Yes, I love *A Christmas Carol*, but it was the recent discovery of a secret book by Charles Dickens that caused me to admire him all the more.

There may be some debate as to whether or not Charles Dickens was a Christian; after all, he was an outspoken critic of the Church of England. But consider this: Can you think of any prophet, or even our Lord Jesus, who wasn't a critic of the Church? A friend recently reminded me of this when I was discussing with her my intent to write about Dickens. She reminded me that it was not a sin to be a critic of the Church, if that criticism is intended to bring about a positive reform or address an area of weakness. Regardless, if there is any question about the faith of Charles Dickens, the following information about his little-known work should bring closure to that question.

The Secret Work of Charles Dickens

In 1849, Charles Dickens wrote a manuscript that included the instruction that it was not to be printed publicly for eighty-five years; honoring his wishes, the book was not published until 1934, after all of his children had died. This book was titled *The Life of Our Lord*; it was written for his children, and its purpose was to communicate to them the importance of a relationship with Christ. To quote Marie Dickens, his daughter-in-law, "This book, the last work of Charles Dickens to be published, has an individual interest and purpose that separate it completely from everything else that Dickens wrote. Quite apart from its Divine Subject, the manuscript is peculiarly personal to the novelist, and is not so much a revelation of his mind as a tribute to his heart and humanity, and also, his deep devotion to Our Lord."

The Life of Our Lord opens with, "My Dear Children, I am very anxious that you should know something about the History of Jesus Christ. For everybody ought to know about Him. No one ever lived who was so good, so kind, so gentle, and so sorry for all people who did wrong, or were in any way ill or miserable, as He was."

Charles Dickens may have been a critic of the Church, but it is clear that he loved Christ, and that he thought it extremely important to pass on that love of Christ to his children—important enough to write a book about the life of Jesus and keep it private for eighty-five years. *The Life of Our Lord* may not be considered orthodox, or even theology that every Protestant would agree with, but it is significant nonetheless, and an important part of our Christian heritage.

C. S. Lewis

My family loved the 2005 movie adaptation of Lewis's book *The Chronicles of Narnia: The Lion, the Witch and the Wardrobe.* I remember my wife and children crying during the scene of Aslan's being killed by the White Witch. How exciting it was to see the resurrected Aslan, who proceeds to breathe life back into those turned to stone by the White Witch and join in the fight to defeat her. In a 1961 letter, Lewis stated that the "whole Narnia story is about Christ." The Narnia series, which has sold over 100 million copies as of 2014, puts forth the power of Christ in a simple-to-understand format that can be enjoyed by both children and adults.

C. S. Lewis was born on November 29, 1898, in Belfast, Ireland, and he died at the age of sixty-four on November 22, 1963. The works of C. S. Lewis are extensive. Including the Narnia series, Lewis authored more than thirty books. Some of his works are *Mere Christianity*, the Space Trilogy series, *The Screwtape Letters*, and *The Great Divorce*. On September 8, 1947, he appeared on the cover of *Time* magazine.

Many people know that C. S. Lewis was an atheist during his younger years. On May 11, 1926, Lewis met J.R.R. Tolkien at a faculty meeting; both were young professors at Oxford University in England at the time. The two of them formed a friendship that would result in the completion of two of the most successful book series ever written: the Chronicles of Narnia series by Lewis and The Lord of the Rings trilogy by Tolkien. Tolkien was instrumental in Lewis's conversion to Christianity, which occurred in September 1931.

The Screwtape Letters

Published in 1942, *The Screwtape Letters* reflects on hypothetical letters between a senior demon, Screwtape, and his nephew, Wormwood. The book is considered a classic and is a must-read for Christians as it gives us a view of human life from the vantage point of Satan, referred to in the book as "Our Father Below." From this satirical work, we can gain an understanding of the methods of Satan to undermine our faith and create division in our midst.

I find it interesting that Lewis proposes as one of the methods that is used by Satan to damage our faith is to encourage us to live in the future and to think little of the past. Lewis writes that "nearly all vices are rooted in the future. Gratitude looks to the past and love to the present; fear, avarice, lust, and ambition look ahead."

Mere Christianity

Published in 1945, *Mere Christianity* is one of the most well-read books that explains the Christian faith. It has been translated into over thirty languages, sold millions of copies, and is frequently given to new believers to help them understand Christian doctrine. Lewis wrote the book in such a way that it would make sense to everyone; a copy was given to me by an adult Sunday school teacher in 1986. I didn't appreciate the gift as much as I should have until years later, but now I highly recommend that every Christian purchase and read a copy. The following are two excerpts from the book.

As long as you are proud you cannot know God. A proud man is always looking down on things and people: and, of course, as long as you are looking down you cannot see something that is above you.

Only those who try to resist temptation know how strong it is.... We never find out the strength of the evil impulse inside us until we try to fight it: and Christ, because He was the only man who never yielded to temptation, is also the only man who knows to the full what temptation means—the only complete realist.

Imagine being a student at Oxford University in 1926 and having the opportunity to converse with both C. S. Lewis and J.R.R. Tolkien and ask them questions. Both had such amazing imaginations. As with Austen and Dickens, the books of Lewis and Tolkien have been made into extremely popular movies. While the Narnia books and movies have very obvious Christian overtones, the movie translations of Tolkien's Lord of the Rings and Hobbit trilogies are not considered by many to have Christian themes, but Tolkien himself would argue otherwise.

J.R.R. Tolkien

The Hobbit, a story that Tolkien had originally written for his children, was almost never published. But the book came to the attention of an employee of George Allen & Unwin, a London publishing company, who persuaded him to submit it for publication. First published in 1937, the book was well-received, and the publisher requested Tolkien write a sequel. Seventeen years later, The Lord of the Rings series was published. The Hobbit and the Lord of the Rings trilogies were made into movies by Peter Jackson, the first being released in 2001, and they are among the most popular movies of all time, combining for a gross box office draw of approximately $5.7 billion as of December 2014. I've seen all six movies, and I loved each of them, but where are the Christian themes?

Tolkien once wrote in a letter to Wheaton College professor Clyde Kilby, "*The Lord of the Rings* is of course a fundamentally religious and Catholic work; unconsciously so at first but consciously in the revision." Tolkien's devout Catholic faith is well-established, but it does take a recognition of the consistent "moral compass" present in the characters. There

147

are recognizable Christian themes present in the books, such as the weak being triumphant over the strong, the power of greed, and one person carrying another's burdens.

A cottage industry has risen of published books that provide faith-based analyses of Tolkien's Hobbit and Lord of the Rings trilogies, including *J.R.R. Tolkien's Sanctifying Myth*, by Bradley Birzer. A review of Birzer's book follows:

> Mr. Birzer's excellent new book is the latest in a bumper crop of studies—including those by Kurt Bruner, Joseph Pearce, Mark Eddy Smith and Jim Ware—that plumb the religious meaning of Middle Earth. Thanks in part to them, it has become increasingly obvious that Tolkien deserves a place alongside T.S. Eliot, Russell Kirk and C.S. Lewis as one of the 20th century's great Christian humanists.
>
> —*John J. Miller, "Myth at the Multiplex,"* Wall Street Journal, *December 2, 2002*

Tolkien was born on January 3, 1892, and he died at the age of eighty-one on September 2, 1973. One little-known fact about him may be his skill as a Bible translator. He translated the book of Jonah, one of my favorites, as part of the Jerusalem Bible, published in 1966.

There can be no doubt of the legacy of Jane Austen, Charles Dickens, C. S. Lewis, and J.R.R. Tolkien. Collectively they are among the greatest British authors who ever lived. Their contributions to our culture are immeasurable, and their place in our Christian heritage is certain. Our children's children will be enjoy their great books in the future. But, like the books of the Bible, their meaning is enhanced when we have an understanding of both the author and the context of the book.

14

Preserving Our Heritage

On July 9, 2014, Islamic State (ISIS) militants destroyed the tomb of the biblical prophet Jonah in Mosul, Iraq; the destruction was video-taped and can be viewed on the Internet today. In only a few months ISIS has killed or displaced hundreds of thousands of people living in Syria and Iraq; they intend to convert, remove, or kill Christians living in any area they control.

On July 11, 2014, Archbishop Louis Raphael Sako I, Iraq's Catholic patriarch, reflected on the consequences related to the destruction of 2,000 years of Christian history in the following statement:

> The next days will be very bad. If the situation does not change, Christians will be left with just a symbolic presence in Iraq... If they leave, their history is finished.

Jews have persevered because they place great importance on documenting their history and teaching their children about their faith. Another reason we should embrace Jewish history is to learn how to preserve our own Christian heritage for the next generation. This is not a "doom and gloom" statement; this is a present-day reality and a work-in-process by a very patient enemy.

What if all records of Judaism and the entire Jewish people were erased from existence? It hasn't happened, but not because of a lack of effort during the last 2,500 years. As Christians, should we care about Judaism? Consider that the history of Christianity overlaps the history of Judaism; if the history of the Jews is erased, it will only be a matter of time before Christian history also begins to be challenged, misrepresented, and erased.

The Jewish people have faced genocide many times, yet they have persevered against severe hostility and persecution. How? What does the Bible say about the preservation of the offspring of Abraham? In Jeremiah 30:11 we read, "'For I am with you,' says the LORD, 'to save you; though I make a full end of all nations where I have scattered you, yet I will not make a complete end of you. But I will correct you in justice, and will not let you go altogether unpunished." The message is that the Jewish people will persevere, even if the countries in which they live do not.

Again, the Jewish people understand the importance of documenting their history and teaching their children about their faith; it is an intentional effort. They have commemorated important dates in their history with celebrations such as Passover, the Day of Atonement, the Day of Pentecost, and Hanukkah, to name a few. Preserving our Christian heritage should include preserving the Jewish heritage. We must be aware of the threats to the preservation of our heritage, which are multiple and worldwide today.

Should Christians care if traces of the Jewish or Christian heritage are lost or destroyed around the world? The Nazis took the same actions during World War II against Jews by destroying their artifacts in an attempt to wipe any memory of them from existence. Make no mistake: A record of your history matters a great deal to the enemy.

The Holocaust

The systematic persecution of the Jews began in Germany during 1933. Between 1933 and the beginning of World War II in 1939, this persecution intensified to the point that Jews were eventually required to wear a yellow Star of David on their clothing. There was pillaging and burning of synagogues, as well.

During World War II, the Nazis attempted to execute their "final solution" regarding the extermination of the entire Jewish people. It is estimated that eleven million people were murdered during the Holocaust; including six million Jews, approximately two-thirds of all Jews living in Europe. The Nazis had not only herded Jews into concentration camps where unthinkable acts were committed, but they had also stolen all of their possessions. The 2014 movie *The Monuments Men* includes a scene in which a barrel of gold tooth fillings was found after being hidden by the Nazis along with rare works of art.

What benefit is there in destroying the Jewish faith? Perhaps it is what it represents; or how the New Testament is linked to the Old Testament. If you wipe out the Jewish people and their history, at some point you may be able to destroy belief in the accuracy and relevance of the Old Testament. And if the history of the Old Testament is destroyed, it becomes much easier to attack the New Testament. We should not hastily disregard this conspiracy theory or think that it is not relevant to a study of the Old Testament.

It is widely known that there are groups of people today who deny the Holocaust ever happened. To quote www.yourish.com:

> When people who are not the president of Iran express doubts that the Holocaust is true, they are called Holocaust deniers. One of the most famous, of course, is David Irving, who lost a libel suit in the U.K. and is currently in prison in Austria for Holocaust denial.

Because of the growing attacks on the history of the Holocaust, websites are being created to defend the accuracy of this horrific event. It is unbelievable that we have to defend such well-documented events, which include eyewitness accounts. Christians in the twenty-first century need to learn from Jews the importance of protecting and preserving their heritage.

God Expelled in a California School

In September 2014, the Springs Charter School in Temecula, California, purged their library of all books with a Christian message, any books written by a Christian author, or any books published by a Christian publishing company. The purge included *The Hiding Place*, the biography of Corrie ten Boom, a Dutch Christian imprisoned by the Nazis for helping Jews escape the Holocaust. The superintendent defended her action in a written response to the Public Justice Institute, saying: "We only keep on our shelves the books that we are authorized to purchase with public funds."

The Hiding Place tells the story of the great courage and faith of a family facing the most severe persecution; it is ironic to think the book has itself become a victim of a secret persecution.

Perhaps we should have our children check their own school libraries to see if *The Hiding Place* is there, or inquire of the local school board to see if Christian-related books have been pulled from our school libraries. The Magna Carta, the Mayflower Compact, the Declaration of Independence, and the Gettysburg Address all make reference to God; would our children benefit from the removal of these documents from our schools?

In response to the school superintendent in California, I would encourage her to check out the Paper Clips Project website. In 1998, eighth graders in Whitwell, Tennessee, began a project to collect paper clips that would represent the lives lost during the Holocaust; the Children's Holocaust Memorial resulted from their efforts. Dedicated in 2001, the memorial includes a rail car from Germany that contains a portion of the more than thirty million paper clips that were collected. In 2004, a documentary entitled *Paper Clips* was released that tells their story.

In November 2013, a Costco store in California was found to have labeled Bibles as "Fiction" instead of "Religion" or "Inspirational." A local pastor who was shopping there discovered this "mistake" and publicized it.

A article dated on November 18, 2013, appeared in the British newspaper *The Telegraph* and quoted former Archbishop of Canterbury, Lord Carey, when he stated that Christianity in Great Britain is just a "generation away from extinction." One response to that declaration from A. N. Wilson the following day stated that there has been a decline of belief, and that "most people simply cannot subscribe to the traditional creeds"—including a virgin birth or a resurrection after death on a cross.

The History Channel regularly airs programs that present history, including "biblical" history, from a non-biblical, non-believer perspective. Perspective means everything when you are presenting a point of view or a position on a topic.

The heart of the prudent acquires knowledge, and the ear of the wise seeks knowledge. —Proverbs 18:15

There is no remembrance of former things, nor will there be any remembrance of things that are to come by those who will come after.
—Ecclesiastes 1:11

Is there any doubt that if we better understood the importance of our Christian heritage, we would do what is necessary to pass it on to our children?

The challenge of history is to recover the past and introduce it to the present.   —*David Thelen*

I did not realize until the last few years that the past was under assault from the present. This assault takes the form of ignorance and apathy, and I myself was part of the problem. I, and other believers, participate in the problem, not because of an inability to learn Christian history, but from a lack of will, or desire, to study Christian history.

History was one of my favorite subjects when I was in school. During my middle school years, I had a wonderful U.S. history teacher who had a passion for the subject. He took us to see *Gone with the Wind* because of its historical significance, and I remember seeing him tear up at times during its viewing. The teacher was African American, and I realized some parts of America's past caused him pain, yet he still wanted the class to see the movie and understand it. Sometimes history reminds us of things we'd like to forget, but we can't ignore events just because they are unpleasant. Neither should we ignore events simply because they relate to Christianity in some way. For example, a U.S. history course should not omit the fact that George Washington prayed during difficult moments during the War for Independence, just because it relates to religion, specifically Christianity.

My U.S. history and government teacher in high school challenged his students to go deeper in the study of past events and to seek to understand history in the context of the times. As an example he challenged us with the question, "What was the primary cause of the Civil War?" I answered "slavery," but the correct answer was actually "state's rights versus federal rights"; Southern states did not have the legal right to secede from the Union. The recent interest in Abraham Lincoln is encouraging; his efforts preserved the Union during the Civil War. Students need to understand the role that Lincoln's faith played in helping him cope with the difficult years of his presidency.

We would also benefit from knowing our own family history. During my freshman year at the University of Tennessee in Knoxville, I was introduced to another passionate teacher of U.S. history. As an extra-credit assignment, he encouraged us to interview a grandparent about the Great Depression and turn in a written report. Up to that point, I had never had much interaction with my grandfather, a self-made millionaire and a very independent man.

My interview with him produced amazing results; his responses related to President Roosevelt's New Deal and the passage of the TVA back in the 1930s were very detailed and opinionated. He had vivid memories of opening his first business and spending his honeymoon in the small room in the back of his store during the Depression era. I think he enjoyed the fact that one of his grandchildren had taken an interest in his past.

Most of my last thirty years has been spent trying to do the right thing—to be a good husband, to be a good father, and to serve my church to the best of my ability. I have sung in the choir, taught Sunday school, served as a deacon and a church treasurer, and chaired several committees, but I wasn't seeking God with the passion He deserved.

> *But without faith it is impossible to please Him, for he who comes to God must believe that He is, and that He is a rewarder of those who diligently seek Him.*
> —Hebrews 11:6

Only in recent years, after I began a passionate, deliberate study of the history of the Bible and the Church, did it become clear to me that the knowledge I was gaining was changing my life. It took several months for me to realize why my life was improving. One reason was that the junk I usually poured into my brain was being replaced with encouraging stories about my Christian ancestors who made a difference in the world. Reading the stories of these men and women in history consumed me, and the causes that inspired them began to inspire me, as well. History that I had once taken for granted, if I even knew about it at all, was now greatly appreciated, and I was compelled to learn more. I was beginning to know what I didn't know, to gain an understanding of where I came from. But I still had a long way to go.

If you've ever seen the movie *Peggy Sue Got Married*, you may better understand what I am talking about. After Peggy Sue goes back in time, she has a greater appreciation for her parents, her sister, her grandparents, her friends, her school, and even her teachers. She energetically sings "My Country 'Tis of Thee" in one scene, while her classmates only mumble the words. In the final scenes of the movie, she seeks and receives sound advice from her grandparents about making good choices in life, making decisions that would make her proud.

In the movie, Peggy Sue's knowledge of her own history plays a major role in her view of the past. She advises the young genius, Richard Norvick, about things to come and tries to warn her boyfriend, and future husband, that his music career would never pan out and would instead later cause years of tension in their marriage.

Peggy Sue Got Married is the story of a woman who would do many things differently if she were given the opportunity. With the benefit of experience, she better understands the importance of a good strudel in keeping the family together and in preserving her heritage.

One major point I took from the movie is that if I could go back and relive parts of my life, accompanied by the experience of the last thirty years, I would invest more of my time in the things that really mattered: spending time with God, reading His Word, and spending time with family and friends. Without a doubt, I would take my faith more seriously and put more time into learning things that really matter. Why? Because it sets the tone for the important decisions, especially those involving marriage, education, career, and children.

In the movie *The Natural*, Glenn Close advises Robert Redford that she believes we live two lives: the one we learn from and the one we live with afterward. We live in a day and age of endless social media, which cannot be denied, but what can be argued is whether or not we are really learning anything meaningful with all these exchanges of thoughts.

Thomas Jefferson once wrote, "A morsel of genuine history is a thing so rare as to be always valuable."

If we fail to teach our children our history, they will have no knowledge of our past other than what they can glean from movies, or worse, misrepresentations of historical events from the media, bestselling books, or even their school textbooks. The less we know about our history, the easier it will be for others to influence us to change our positions on important matters, or worse, we become indifferent to the world around us. The less we know about failed sociological, political, and governmental theories, the more likely we are to embrace or accept repackaged versions of them in the future.

Some people want to forget, ignore, or even rewrite huge portions of the Bible, or they deny the fact that various people ever lived, despite strong evidence to the contrary. Are we witnessing the growth of nihilism? The definition of the term follows, and it seems to characterize a growing belief system in the world today.

Nihilism is the belief that all values are baseless and that nothing can be known or communicated....Nihilism is most often associated with

155

Friedrich Nietzsche, who argued that its corrosive effects would eventually destroy all moral, religious, and metaphysical convictions and precipitate the greatest crisis in human history.
—*Internet Encyclopedia of Philosophy*

Who would benefit from such a belief as nihilism? What motive would any sane person have to see the destruction of moral convictions or religious beliefs? And is this really a new way of thinking?

Now the serpent was more cunning than any beast of the field which the LORD *God had made. And he said to the woman, "Has God indeed said, 'You shall not eat of every tree of the garden'?"*   —Genesis 3:1

The Genesis 3 Attack

This attack has never changed. From the time of Adam, Abraham, Moses, and David —all the way to the present day… The world has used the Genesis 3 attack to reject God's moral code for our own self-seeking pleasure… Today the Genesis 3 attack is vehemently directed at the book of Genesis. If God didn't really give us a reliable history, then how can we believe He has given us a reliable Savior?
—*Steve Ham,* Answers in Genesis, *October 14, 2010*

Perhaps a study of history does not sound appealing at first. We might have more interest in history if the medium used to communicate the subject was entertaining. Popular historical movies include *Lincoln*, the miniseries *The Bible, Schindler's List, Saving Private Ryan*, and *The Passion of the Christ*; there are many others. A controversial movie about Noah's ark, starring Russell Crowe, was released in 2014, as well as a movie about Moses. We enjoy fictional stories mixed with a little history, such as *Forrest Gump*, *National Treasure*, and *The Da Vinci Code*. The trouble with these movies is that some people might believe them to be historically accurate.

I once watched a documentary about a "monster shark" on the Discovery Channel, and ended up getting new material supporting the thesis of this book. It provided another example of why we can't always rely on television or movies for our history education. The documentary was *Megalodon: The Monster Shark Lives*, which first aired during August 2013.

The film was marketed and presented as a documentary based on true evidence. But the Discovery Channel had hired actors to play scientists, and for the most part, the film reflected a fabrication of facts.

The Discovery Channel defended the film, referring to a notice that flashed during the last minutes of the show explaining that *Megalodon* was a film about a legend, not a scientifically proven documentary. I watched most of the film, thinking it was a documentary, but I missed the disclaimer that quickly flashed at the end. This should remind us that even the Discovery Channel and the History Channel sometimes air programming that is actually drama presented as fact, or that represents opinions and theories they happen to agree with. In the case of *Megalodon*, they may simply be attempting to create interest in the film and they are willing to mislead the viewer to do so.

Once the show aired and viewers realized the film had no basis in fact, but was only legend and speculation, they were outraged. One viewer commented, "Thanks, Discovery, for making me doubt anything and everything you've ever done." But despite the protests, I believe the "mocu-mentary" is here to stay, and that it represents the new standard of education in America: no basis in fact, no way to prove the theories presented. The main objective seems to be to find something different from Scripture.

Pointing out the flaws in the presentation of the pseudo-documentary *Megalodon* is not difficult; even fans of the Discovery Channel were angry over the use of this fabricated film to kick off "Shark Week." Hopefully, the network will think twice before promoting fiction as fact in the future. The bigger problem occurs when a well-written novel contains just enough facts to make people challenge their beliefs in very important matters, as evidenced by the popularity of *The Da Vinci Code*, by Dan Brown.

The Da Vinci Code

This novel was marketed as being well-researched and having a background based entirely on fact. The *Boston Globe* called it a "delightful display of erudition" (*erudition* is defined as "extensive knowledge acquired chiefly from books; profound, recondite, or bookish learning"). Did Dan Brown think his book was historically accurate?

I began the research for *The Da Vinci Code* as a skeptic. I entirely expected, as I researched the book, to disprove this (Jesus/Mary Magdeline/Grail) theory. And after numerous trips to Europe and about two years of research I really became a believer. I decided the theory makes more sense to me than what I learned as a child.

—*Dan Brown, ABC TV Special, 2003*

On June 9, 2003, on the *Today* show, in response to Matt Lauer's question, "How much of this is based on reality in terms of things that actually occurred?" Dan Brown's declaration was, "Absolutely all of it."

On June 23, 2005, the *National Geographic* released a survey of Canadian readers of *The Da Vinci Code.* Thirty-two percent of the 1,005 adults surveyed agreed with the novel's claim that Jesus had founded a "bloodline" that is protected by a secret society to this day. In May 2006 the British pollster Opinion Research Business conducted a similar survey, discovering that out of one thousand people surveyed, 60 percent of the readers of the novel believed Jesus had had a child by Mary Magdalene, as opposed to 30 percent of people who had not read the book.

In an October 23, 2005, interview on CNN with Martin Savidge, when asked, "How much is true and how much is fabricated?" Brown's response was, "Ninety-nine percent of it is true...all that is fiction is...Robert Langdon, and all of his action is fictionalized. But the background is true."

Considering the phenomenal success of the book, can we really ask whether it matters that people believe *The Da Vinci Code* over the Bible or documented history? Did Dan Brown put as much work into his research as the translators of the Old and New Testaments did? Has Mr. Brown uncovered lost documents that support the suppositions set forth in the novel?

Several websites and books repudiate the "history" presented in *The Da Vinci Code*, including a website created by Tim O'Neill, located at historyversusthedavincicode.com, and the nonfiction book *The Real History Behind the Da Vinci Code* by Sharan Newman. It is interesting that even non-Christians took an interest in challenging the historical accuracy of Dan Brown's novel and discrediting it. The question is, however, has the damage already been done?

Does it even matter whether there are bestselling books or entertaining films and websites that portray history in a skewed or baseless manner, void of fact? To quote Tim O'Neill, "That depends on how much importance you place on a clear understanding of history…"

Obviously, my thinking is that it matters a great deal that we have a clear understanding of history. With our culture attached to a feeding tube of misinformation and false history, it has never been more important to receive a healthy dose of time-tested, documented history.

This book contains morsels of history that, once digested, will allow you to make the connection to a common bond shared with all Christians that unites us. Christians share a connection with the early Church and a heritage with Israel through the Old Testament. Understanding this connection will strengthen your faith.

When you begin to understand something at a deeper level, your passion for it begins to brew. —*Entrepreneur magazine, 2003*

Delusion about history is a serious matter; it can gravely affect the history that is waiting to be made. —*John Terraine*

It is a great pity that every human being does not, at an early age of his life, have to write a historical book. He would then realize that the human race is in quite a jam about the truth. —*Rebecca West*

I am in strong agreement with Rebecca West regarding the human race being "in quite a jam about the truth," but the truth is not always easy to find. As a CPA, I have learned the common practice of digging deep to obtain critical information in order to prepare an accurate financial statement. There is a humorous saying about numbers: "Figures don't lie, but liars can figure."

Developing a discipleship class on the history of the English Bible led me to a renewed interest in my Christian heritage. I considered purchasing an antique Bible and even priced several of them online. The website selling them (www.greatsite.com) had a great deal of information about each book's history. I purchased *A Visual History of the English Bible* by Donald Brake, a collector and an authority on the subject. This book communicates his love of God's Word. I believe every Christian should have some knowledge related to the history of the Bible so that they will know when it is being misrepresented.

There was a time when the Bible was used not only as the basis for teaching history in the United States, but even in most of the world. Whether we even agree with its teachings or not, there is great historical significance in God's Word. The world, including the Church in America, no longer holds the Bible in the high esteem it once did. Are we better off?

Preserving Christian heritage begins with an understanding of the history of the Bible itself. The Bible was the first book ever printed, has been translated into over 2,400 languages, and is the bestselling book of all time. Countless numbers of people have died over the centuries in order to make God's Word available to us. We must be reminded from time to time of the human price that was paid to keep this history from being forgotten.

We preserve our heritage by reviving interest in the Bible.

There is much at stake; our knowledge of history will play a significant role in our ability to make important decisions.

If you want to understand today, you have to search yesterday.
—*Pearl S. Buck*

History is a vast early warning system.　　　—*Norman Cousins*

Will our Christian heritage survive the Information Age? With so much at stake; we must open our eyes to the immediate need for change.

What is necessary to change a person is to change his awareness of himself.　　　—*Abraham Maslow*

An increased understanding of Christian history has renewed and strengthened my faith in God and given me a quiet confidence that, no matter what happens, God is in control.

Harvard University was founded with the goal of training ministers, and it took up John 17:3 as its primary goal:

And this is eternal life, that they may know You, the only true God, and Jesus Christ whom You have sent.

The original motto of Harvard University was—in Latin—"Truth for Christ and the Church"; in the twentieth century the motto was reduced to simply "Truth." At Harvard, as at most universities in the United States, the teaching of God's Word is all but gone, or not allowed.

Over the last fifty years, the teaching of the Scriptures has been diminished or even removed from public schools, and, sadly, even in His Church. The study of the Scriptures is often replaced with good advice, short stories, or a mixture of light scripture with clever dialogue. A byproduct of our decreased study of the Scriptures is a poor understanding of God and a weak and unfulfilled relationship with Him.

The study of history is an important element of our basic education. Yet since the time I was in school, the study of history is receiving a diminishing role in the required curriculum. My wife attended school in the state of Virginia from 1967 through 1979, and she was required to take Virginia and U.S. history in the fourth grade, and then U.S. history again in eleventh grade. The following quote from Dr. Ben Carson describes perfectly another of my motives for writing this book:—to inform and educate:

> Education is such a fundamental principle to the success of America and we're allowing it to go under. You go out and talk to the average person out there and they may be able to tell you who won Dancing with the Stars or who won the football game, but they can't tell you anything important, they don't know about foreign policy and they don't know about the way our government works. Consequently, they have become the ignorant, they have become the unprepared. This is exactly what the founders of this country warned against, they said, "Our system of government is based upon a well-educated and informed populace. And if our populace ever becomes anything other than that, we will become a different country." They knew what they were talking about. —*Dr. Ben Carson*

I recently became aware of the Dreyfuss Initiative, spearheaded by Academy Award–winning actor Richard Dreyfuss. This effort has nothing to do with religion, but I appreciate his passion to teach our children civics and a basic knowledge of the foundational principles upon which the government of the United States is based. A summary of the Dreyfuss Initiative from its website, www.thedreyfussinitiative.org, is found below:

Civic education is the founding mandate of public education. Free public schools were developed in America for the express purpose of raising up good citizenship. This purpose has been abandoned and must be regained. Thus the mission of The Initiative is to create a demand for a more expert learning experience and to give our kids the splendid pleasure of learning what power they have.

During an appearance on Mike Huckabee's talk show in May 2014, Mr. Dreyfuss made the following comments.

> We were responsible for the greatest revolution in the history of civilization. We gave to 98 percent of the human race freedoms that they have been lashed for, lost fingers for, or had their heads chopped off for, and we gave it to them for free and we are the most revolutionary nation that has ever been and ever will be and we don't know enough about our constitution or our history to know why we should be proud of it.
>
> George Washington said the Constitution should be central, the party should be peripheral. Now we've got it all backed around and now the parties are central and the constitution is peripheral. We don't know anything about why the Constitution is the most single greatest step toward humans improving civilization since the beginning of man's sojourn on earth.

We have seen a dramatic shift in the culture of the United States during the last few years, but is that a good thing? Will my children's children be better off because of the decisions and choices Americans are making today?

Consider the following verses:

Again, the kingdom of heaven is like a merchant seeking beautiful pearls, who, when he had found one pearl of great price, went and sold all that he had and bought it. —Matthew 13:45–46

Ask, and it will be given to you; seek, and you will find; knock, and it will be opened to you. For everyone who asks receives, and he who seeks finds, and to him who knocks it will be opened. —Matthew 7:7–8

Even if we weren't Christians, the subject of this book should be compelling for purely educational reasons. Consider that the Bible was the first printed book in history, and the best-selling book of all time. In the movie *The Day After Tomorrow*, there is a scene where the group trapped in the New York Public Library is burning books to stay warm. One of them is holding a Gutenberg Bible and won't give it up. He is asked if he thinks it will save him. He responds by telling them that although he does not believe in God, the book represents the dawn of the Age of Reason, which he believes to be mankind's greatest achievement. In other words, man began the Age of Reason by producing the first printed Bible.

If every book, or record of books, were to be destroyed, save one book of your choice, which book would it be? Is there any book that has more significance than the Bible? Despite all the criticisms of the Bible in today's culture, a deliberate study of God's Word will reveal that He has great intentions for us and that He loves us more than we can imagine. Why would we not want to revive a history that includes the encouraging words that follow?

> *But those who hope in the LORD will renew their strength, they will soar on wings of eagles; they will run and not grow weary, they will walk and not be faint.* —Isaiah 40:31 NIV

Whether you are a person of faith, no faith, lukewarm faith, or just an interested bystander, the question of God's existence and the relevance of His written Word cannot be ignored. We can't discount the relevance of the Bible and ignore it simply because we want nothing to do with religion or Christianity. To quote bestselling author Josh McDowell, *"The evidence demands a verdict!"*

A dear friend of my wife was once overheard counseling a friend of hers to take his child to church. The friend stated he was not a believer and did not want to be a hypocrite, so he was not going to take his child to church. The response of my wife's dear friend was profound when she replied, "What are you going to tell your child one day, when you are both in the pits of hell, and the child asks you, 'Daddy, why didn't you ever tell me there was another way?'"

I think about the millions of readers of *The Da Vinci Code* who, after reading it, no longer believe in the biblical account of Christ. There are other books, movies, and websites claiming to discredit history as recorded in God's Word, having little basis in fact, or worse, based on complete fabrications.

After consideration is given to the importance of the Old Testament to Christianity, how can we do anything but embrace it and work to preserve it? It is the foundation of our history and our heritage. The fact that the Jewish people have survived centuries of persecution is a testament to the power of preserving your heritage.

If there remains any doubt about the importance of our Christian heritage, I encourage you to watch the movie *The Book of Eli*. With the exception of some brutality and bad language (the movie is rated R), this movie is an excellent reflection of a world on the verge of losing any record of God's holy Word. If darkness is defined as the absence of light, imagine a world in which the Bible no longer exists. Utter darkness.

15

Lessons from "The Obsolete Man"

Believers face challenges to their faith every day. Rejoice and be glad! Without challenges, we would never grow, seek the truth, or turn to God in prayer. Iron sharpens iron. In AD 197, Tertullian wrote that "the blood of martyrs is the seed of the Christians." This was in response to the severe Roman persecution of Christians, but the persecution only resulted in an increase in their numbers. When believers stand on their faith, it inspires others to do the same.

Over thirty years ago, I was challenged by my college English Masterpieces professor. Because of that challenge I faced the truth that I didn't know what I didn't know. The lack of knowledge of my Christian history prevented me from understanding important Christian literature, such as *Sir Gawain and the Green Knight*. I had a poor understanding of the Jewish, Catholic, and other Protestant faiths. In short, my faith suffered from a poor understanding of my Christian heritage.

In the chapters of this book, we have considered inspiring stories about believers whose actions changed history. But what if we were to do nothing about them? What if we decided that our Christian heritage is really not an essential element of our faith, or what if our history was to be lost to the next generation? Rod Serling may have had that future in mind when he wrote "The Obsolete Man."

On June 2, 1961, episode 65 of *The Twilight Zone* aired for the first time. It starred the late Burgess Meredith and was titled "The Obsolete Man." The topics covered in this episode sound like something out of a college-level theology class, including euthanasia and totalitarianism. What high expectations the producers had back in 1961, with respect to the audience's ability to understand and comprehend the story.

The complex themes covered in "The Obsolete Man" include Orwellian totalitarianism, a belief in God, and euthanasia. Interestingly there are two

165

versions of this episode available on YouTube. One version is the full-length episode; the second version removes any references to God. Is that not ironic and consistent with the theme of this book, not to mention the television episode itself? So, what is the theme of "The Obsolete Man"?

The setting is sometime in the future, and the form of government is a totalitarian state. The main character, Romney Wordsworth (Meredith), has been placed on trial for the crime of being obsolete. His occupation of librarian is obsolete, as the State has eliminated books. A second crime, punishable by death, is that he believes in God; the State claims to have proven there is no God.

The chancellor prosecutes Mr. Wordsworth because he is not considered to be an asset to the State and therefore must be liquidated. Wordsworth is found guilty and convicted, but he is allowed to choose his method of execution. He requests a personal assassin to whom he may privately disclose his method of execution and that his execution be televised. The court, thinking it will be quite a spectacle and leave an impression on the audience, teaching them the consequences of having no use to the State, grants both requests.

Cameras are installed in Wordsworth's apartment; the chancellor arrives at 11:16 P.M. and is told that the chosen method of execution is by an explosive set to go off at midnight. Wordsworth explains to the chancellor that the execution will be of interest to the public as the door to his room is locked and the chancellor will die along with him at midnight. The intention is to show the public how a spiritual man faces death. He then pulls out his illegal copy of the Bible and reads Psalm 23. The chancellor begins to panic as midnight nears, while the librarian, who believes in God, remains calm. As the final minutes tick away, the chancellor begs Wordsworth to allow him to leave, even calling on the God that he did not believe existed. Wordsworth responds that for the sake of his God, he would open the door. The chancellor is allowed to leave the room moments before the bomb explodes, killing Wordsworth. The whole nation has witnessed the interaction between Wordsworth and the chancellor.

The chancellor returns to the courtroom to discover he has been found to be obsolete. The court informs him that he had disgraced the state and had no courage. The chancellor, like Wordsworth, has been judged to be obsolete.

In his closing comments, Rod Serling commented that any state or ideology that failed to recognize the dignity or the worth of man was obsolete. The entity worshipped by the chancellor believed that there was no God. Books had also been eliminated.

This episode is intended to teach a strong political lesson, but to me the lessons are spiritual. The conversation between Wordsworth and the chancellor includes a reference to Stalin and Hitler, with Wordsworth asking why the chancellor had failed to learn anything from history. The chancellor responded by stating that Stalin and Hitler were not wrong, but they had simply failed to accomplish their objectives.

I once thought that Stephen Covey's *Seven Habits of Highly Effective People* should be required for every senior to help prepare them for dealing with life after high school. To that I would now add a course that includes viewing the full-length episode of "The Obsolete Man," followed by several hours of discussion as to its meaning.

So, what lessons should we take away from "The Obsolete Man"? For me, learning lessons from history implies that we are teaching history to our children, which includes raising the bar of our Christian education. I'm not talking about Christian private schools that already place an emphasis on important events in Christian history; I mean in the church around the corner. I've heard it said that "Sunday school is the only school where you never get tested or graduate."

Another lesson learned is from the dignity the librarian exhibited as he accepted his fate. He made his point and even showed mercy to the chancellor, and his point was made to the audience. When it comes time to die, will we cry out to a merciful God with whom we have a relationship, or will we be terrified as we move on to nothingness or a possible hell?

A third lesson is the consequences of a failure to learn from history. Related to the first lesson, it is one thing not to teach history to our children, but it is another thing to fail to learn any lessons from the past. The Old Testament is full of accounts of people failing to remember their past or to learn from it.

The final lesson is that we should be wary to ensure that the Bible and the worship of God are not outlawed in the United States. As mentioned earlier, Miriam Ibrahim, who was pregnant when she was first jailed in February 2014, was sentenced to death in Sudan for the crime of being a Christian. She was ready to die rather than renounce her faith; her execution was to take place after the birth of her child. Her courage should serve as an example to us all. Would you give up your faith if your life depended on it?

Tramp for the Lord

Do you know the story of Corrie ten Boom? Her parents hid Jews in their home in Holland during World War II. They were betrayed in February 1944, and the Gestapo raided their home and arrested her entire family. The ten Boom family was not Jewish; they were Christians. In her autobiography, *The Hiding Place*, Corrie ten Boom told of the dying words of her Aunt Jans: "Dear Jesus, I thank you that we must come with empty hands, I thank you that you have done all—all on the cross, and that all we need in life or death, is to be sure of this."

Prior to the arrest of her family, a local rabbi brought the tomes of Jewish theology, a large collection of books, to Casper ten Boom for protection. The rabbi told Casper, "Books do not age as you and I do. They will speak still when we are gone, to generations we will never see. Yes, the books must survive." The rabbi would later be taken by the Nazis, but the books survived.

Corrie ten Boom miraculously survived the Nazi death camp and later started a worldwide ministry. Her book *Tramp for the Lord* is an amazing book that chronicles her ministry of healing and forgiveness. Her autobiography *The Hiding Place* was a bestseller in the early 1970s, and it was made into a movie by World Wide Pictures (a Billy Graham organization). It is absurd to think that a public school would ever intentionally pull her books off of their shelves, but this is why Christians need to stay informed.

How Then Shall We Live?

One of my favorite Christmas songs is "I Heard the Bells on Christmas Day." The words are taken from a poem written by Henry Wadsworth Longfellow during the Civil War, but they speak to me loudly and clearly today.

And in despair I bowed my head;
There is no peace on earth, I said;
For hate is strong, and mocks the song
Of peace on earth, good-will to men!

Then pealed the bells more loud and deep:
"God is not dead, nor doth He sleep;
The Wrong shall fail, The Right prevail,
With peace on earth, good-will to men."

The Christian response to the bad news of the day should be similar to that of the apostle Paul: During the time he was in prison, he sang. We can sing praises to our God and King, and we should have a revival—a revival of our faith and our heritage. It is that simple. Christians should ready themselves, put on the "full armor of God," and always be ready to give a reason for their hope (see 1 Peter 3:15).

History is history, as unpleasant as it may be. The Trail of Tears is not a happy story. Christians experienced horrific deaths at the hands of Nero and other Roman leaders. This book has covered several events in history that are not proud moments for American culture. But how do we help preserve history if we distort it? I applaud Steven Spielberg for making the movie *Schindler's List* in 1993, an important story of courage that must be remembered.

In one of the final scenes of the movie, Oskar Schindler is leaving his factory; he must leave before the Allies arrive or risk being tried as a war criminal. His Jewish friends are urging him to leave and thanking him for risking his life to save them, but Schindler is not feeling good about his efforts to save as many as he could. (Approximately 1,200 were saved.) But Oskar Schindler is heartbroken that more lives were not saved. He felt that he could have worked harder to save even one more life during the Holocaust. He died penniless, but he changed the world for those he saved. Could one of us be the next Oskar Schindler in the world? I compare that scene to when we will face Christ and be asked to give an account of our lives on earth. Did we run a good race, or will we be ashamed that we did not do more while we had the time, thinking it would make little or no difference?

The Monuments Men

George Clooney's 2014 movie, *The Monuments Men*, chronicles the story of several soldiers who were given the mission of saving historic paintings, statues, and works of fine art from Hitler during World War II. These men had the mission of finding and preserving treasures from the past. During the effort to save these treasures, several men were killed. After the war was over, the question was asked of the leader of the mission, played by Clooney, as to whether the recovered art was worth the lives of the men who died during the mission. Of course we know it was, as several million pieces of art were recovered, much of which was related to Christian history. We must protect the links to our past, not only the paintings and statues, but the letters and documents that reflect the truth of our past. This movie communicates well the importance of preserving history for the benefit of the next generation.

From Generation to Generation

And His mercy is on those who fear Him from generation to generation.
—Luke 1:50

This will be written for the generation to come,that a people yet to be created may praise the LORD. —Psalm 102:18

One generation shall praise Your works to another, and shall declare Your mighty acts. —Psalm 145:4

I received more evidence of the need for this book while listening to a radio talk show around 3:00 P.M. on May 17, 2014, as I was returning home from a vacation. On this radio talk show, World War II and Vietnam War veterans were being interviewed. The WWII veteran had fought at Iwo Jima, one of the bloodiest battles of the war, and he had been asked some questions by his grandson. During the course of the interview, his grandson shared his understanding of World War II—that the United States had started the war by bombing Japan! The veteran had to set his grandson straight and explain Japan's surprise attack on Pearl Harbor, which the grandson had not been taught about in school.

It is worth repeating, perspective means everything when teaching history. Christians with school-age children need to understand that there is a war in progress to change how history is taught in the public school system, and the outcome may actually change our heritage.

As Christians, we have a Protestant, Catholic, and Jewish heritage. Our history includes men and women whose faith prevented them from doing nothing when God called them to act. From Abraham to King David; from Mary, the mother of Jesus, to the apostle Paul; from Saint Jerome to Gutenberg; from Martin Luther to Billy Graham—we share a common history. Our ancestors include Desiderius Erasmus, Charles Dickens, Corrie ten Boom, Martin Luther King Jr., and countless others. How much stronger is our faith when we link arms with them?

Think of your Christian heritage as a chain; each believer is a link in that chain. Imagine that our understanding of our Christian history measures the strength of each link. When we have knowledge of the essential elements of our Christian heritage, we strengthen our own link in the chain. We benefit from the experiences and wisdom of believers who lived before us.

Lois Lowry's book, *The Giver*, tells the story of a world in which one person is entrusted with the memories (the history) of their world. The Giver is asked by his protégé, "Why do you and I have to hold these memories?" "It gives us wisdom," the Giver replies. We can be the seed of the next great generation of believers and the generation that connects our children to their Christian heritage.

Embracing our Christian history can only strengthen our faith. Imagine families, churches, and denominations united by their common heritage. A unified Christian church could change the world.

Our history leads back to Christ, back to Abraham, and back to Adam. How firm a foundation our faith has when it includes the understanding of our brothers and sisters whose faith made a difference in the world. My prayer is that we will be the seed of a revival of our Christian heritage for the next generation. As our God has instructed in His Word, we must remember Him—we must remember where we came from.

The people and events you have read about in this book are a part of your Christian heritage, a part of the story of us. Our challenge is to remember that God can, and will, use ordinary people like us to continue making history.

You matter to God. What you do with your history determines the future of your children.

The ultimate test of a moral society
is the kind of world
that it leaves to its children.

—*Dietrich Bonhoeffer*

Sources

"Ark of the Covenant," at www.ark-of-the-covenant.com, 2013.

"Council of Nicea and The Da Vinci Code," at www.religionfacts.com/da_vinci_code/nicea.htm.

"How Did Canonization of the New Testament Happen?" at www.toughquestionsanswered.org, 2012.

"Nero Persecutes the Christians, AD 64—Eyewitness to History," at www.eyewitnesstohistory.com, 2000.

Anders, Max. *30 Days to Understanding the Bible.*

Bobrick, Benson. *Wide as the Waters.*

Brake, Donald. *A History of the English Bible.*

Christianity: The Illustrated Guide to 2,000 Years of the Christian Faith (Millennium House).

Curtis, A. Kenneth, J. Stephen Lang, and Randy Petersen. *The 100 Most Important Events in Christian History.*

Denton, Michael. *Evolution: A Theory in Crisis (Burnett Books, 1985), 66.*

Foxe, John. *Foxe's Book of Martyrs.*

Hill, Jonathan. *Handbook to the History of Christianity (Zondervan).*

Horton, David, *ed., The Portable Seminary (2006).*

Http://facts.randomhistory.com/2009/06/09_black-death.htm.

Http://www.historymakers.info/inspirational-christians/william-tyndale.html.

Http://www.kingjamesbibletranslators.org.

Morris, Henry. *The Long War Against God (Master Books, 2000).*

Parker, D. C. *CODEX SINAITICUS (2010).*

Perry, John. *10 Christians Everyone Should Know (Thomas Nelson, 2012).*

Reynolds, John Mark, *ed., The Great Books Reader—Excerpts and Essays on the Most Influential Books in Western Civilization.*

Stone, Larry. *The Story of the Bible.*

Teems, David. *Majestie—The King Behind the King James Bible.*

The Rose Book of Bible Charts, Maps, and Timelines.

Torrey, *The Fundamentals, Volume III (Baker Books).*

www.americanchristianhistory.com.

www.christianitytoday.com.

www.civilwar.org.

www.douglasgilliland.com/faith/calvin/1_main.htm.

www.faithology.com/biographies/desiderius-erasmus.

www.greatamericanhistory.net.

www.heritage.org.

www.monticello.org.

www.Septuagint.net.

www.standingthegap.org/Septuagint.

www.thedreyfussiniative.org.

www.ukapologetics.net.

www.wallbuilders.com.

Stepping Stones: A Timeline

BC 4000—Approximate date God creates Adam and Eve

BC 2348—Noah's flood

BC 2166—Abraham is born

BC 2005—Jacob and Esau are born

BC 1876—Jacob (Israel) moves his family to Egypt

BC 1446—The first Passover, the Exodus, the Ten Commandments

BC 1011—The reign of King David begins

BC 971—The reign of King Solomon begins

BC 950—King Solomon's Temple is completed

BC 931—The nation of Israel is divided into the Northern (Israel) and Southern (Judah) Kingdoms

BC 722—The Northern Kingdom (Israel) falls to the Assyrians

BC 612—The city of Nineveh is destroyed

BC 586—The Southern Kingdom (Judah) falls to Babylon, Jerusalem and Solomon's Temple are destroyed

BC 516—The Jews return from seventy-year exile; the Temple is rebuilt

BC 255—The Septuagint is translated in Alexandria, Egypt

BC 63—Jerusalem is conquered by Pompey for Rome

BC 6–4—Jesus is born (approximate date)

AD 6—Judea becomes a Roman province

AD 29—Jesus begins His public ministry

AD 33—Jesus is crucified, resurrected, and appears for forty days

AD 35—Paul is converted

AD 41—Believers are first called "Christians" at Antioch

AD 64—The great fire in Rome; Nero blames Christians

AD 66–70—Roman soldiers lay siege to Jerusalem and destroy the Second Temple; one wall remains standing, known today as the Western Wall

AD 155—Polycarp, bishop of Smyrna, is burned at the stake at the age of eighty-six

AD 251—Cyprian writes On Unity of the Church

AD 261—First church buildings are constructed as rectangular buildings

AD 303–304—Christians are persecuted severely under Diocletian, who burns scriptures and kills thousands

AD 312—Constantine becomes the emperor of Rome, is considered to be the first Christian emperor, and ends persecution of Christians

AD 324—Eusebius writes Church History

AD 330—Capital of Roman Empire is moved to Constantinople

AD 367—The twenty-seven books of the New Testament are listed and confirmed for the first time by Athanasius, bishop of Alexandria

AD 405—Jerome completes the Vulgate

AD 432—Patrick evangelizes Ireland

AD 476—The Western Roman Empire falls, recognized as the beginning of the Middle Ages

AD 610—Muhammad claims to be a prophet of God

AD 800—Egbert unifies England and becomes its first king; approximate date of the Book of Kells

AD 988—Vladimir is converted, bringing Christianity to Russia

AD 999—Leif Erikson converts to Christianity

1054—The Great Schism divides the Eastern Church (the Orthodox Church in Constantinople) and the Western Church (the Catholic Church in Rome)

1066—The Norman conquest of England

1095–1272—The Christian Crusades

1209—Saint Francis of Assisi renounces his wealth

1215—The signing of the Magna Carta

1266—Kublai Khan requests 100 Christian teachers

1337–1453—The Hundred Years War

1348–51—The Bubonic plague kills an estimated 75 to 200 million people

1382—John Wycliffe translates the Bible from the Latin Vulgate into English: the first English Bible

1453—Constantinople falls to the Ottoman Turks, the Hagia Sophia is converted from a Christian church to a mosque

1456—Johann Gutenberg produces the first printed book, a Latin Bible, the Vulgate, using movable type

1492—Columbus discovers America

1516—Desiderius Erasmus publishes a Greek translation of the New Testament, Erasmus's translations form the Textus Receptus, the "received text," which is the basis of the New Testament in the King James Bible

1517—October 31, Martin Luther posts his 95 Theses on the door of the Castle Church in Wittenberg, marking the beginning of the Protestant Reformation

1535—Henry VIII breaks from the Roman Catholic Church

1536—William Tyndale is burned at the stake, John Calvin publishes Institutes on the Christian Religion

1537—King Henry VII permits distribution of English Bible

1558—Queen Elizabeth I takes the throne of England

1572—August, the Saint Bartholomew's Day Massacre

1605—November 5, Gunpowder Plot in England

1609—The first Baptist church meets in Holland

1610—The Douay-Rheims Bible is published

1611—The King James Version is completed

1620—The Mayflower Compact is signed

1621—The first Thanksgiving is celebrated

1663—The first Bible is printed in North America

1738—John Wesley's conversion experience

1776—The Declaration of Independence is signed

1782—The United States Congress endorses the Bible for general use

1816—Richard Allen founds the African Methodist Episcopal Church

1859—Darwin's Origin of the Species is published

1925—Scope's "Monkey Trial" takes place in Dayton, Tennessee

1933—Hitler is elected chancellor of Germany

1947—The Dead Sea Scrolls are discovered, the Jewish State of Israel is recognized

1961—"The Obsolete Man" first airs

1962—Engel versus Vitale takes place, the Supreme Court rules to remove prayer from public schools

1973—Roe versus Wade takes place, the Supreme Court rules to legalize abortion on demand

About the Author

TOMMY DAUGHERTY is a Certified Public Accountant with over thirty years of experience in his profession. He is committed to excellence and accuracy in the analysis of information and reporting of financial data. Thirty years ago, a college professor challenged his understanding of Christianity during a study of *Sir Gawain and the Green Knight*. The professor made it clear that the student didn't know what he didn't know. Three years ago Tommy was led on a journey to gain a deeper understanding of his Christian heritage, and a new world was opened to him. *Why Your History Matters* represents the sharing of that journey and a call to arms that this generation may be in danger of failing to pass their Christian heritage on to the next.

To contact the author, write him at his office at
4421 Whittle Springs Rd., Ste B, Knoxville, TN 37917.
Or send him an email at info@dcpllc.org.

Visit his website at:
http://WhyYourHistoryMatters.com

Notes

Notes

Notes

Notes